Contents

Foreword

by W. Edwards Deming

The economic position of the U. S. has been on the decline for three decades. The prevailing system of management has brought waste and high costs. We have been led astray by faith in adversarial competition. One could easily cite examples of wasteful practices:

Short-term thinking. Maintain the price of the company's stock.

Rank people, teams, salesmen, divisions, with reward at the top, punishment at the bottom.

Ranking people has led to the so-called annual appraisal of people. The result is conflict, demoralization, lower productivity, lower quality, suppression of innovation.

Management by results. Take immediate action on any fault, mistake, defect, complaint, delay, accident, breakdown. Certainly we need good results, but action initiated by a result (action on the last data-point) only guarantees more trouble in the future. This is tampering, the cause of which is failure to understand the distinction between common causes of variation, and special causes.

It is a mistake to suppose that if you can not measure the results of an activity, you can not manage it. The fact is that the most important losses and gains can not be measured, yet for survival they must be managed. We have just spelled out some examples.

Most of the wasteful practices of the prevailing system of management are wrong ways to manage people. They begin with grades in school, from toddlers on up through the university. They lead to the annual appraisal of people on the job, even of teachers; incentive pay; monetary reward for suggestions; bonuses (to make sure that somebody does his job); quotas for production; gains from training, gains from education; business plans based on competitive measures.

Management addressed toward optimization of a system would offer improvement. A system must have an aim. Without an aim, there is no system.

A system must be managed. The bigger the system, the more difficult it is to manage it for optimization.

The performance of any component within a system is to be judged in terms of its contribution to the aim of the system, not for its individual production or profit, nor for any other competitive measure.

Optimization of a system should be the basis of negotiation between any two people, between divisions of a company, between customer and supplier, between countries, between competitors. Everybody gains under optimization.

Best efforts and hard work will not suffice, nor new machinery, computers, automation, gadgets. One could well add that we are being ruined by best efforts put forth with the best intentions but without guidance of a theory of management for optimization of a system. There is no substitute for knowledge.

The change requires transformation, change of state -- metamorphosis -- in industry, education, and government. The transformation will restore the individual by abolishment of grades in school on up through the university; by abolishment of the annual appraisal of people on the job, M.B.O., quotas for production, incentive pay, competition between people, competition between divisions, and other forms of sub-optimization. The transformation is not stamping out fires, solving problems, nor cosmetic improvements.

The transformation must be led by people that acquire profound knowledge. Mr. Scherkenbach is one who puts profound knowledge into action for continual improvement of quality of product, quality of service, improvement of education, and improvement of government. The book is notable for clarity of principles, bountifully illustrated by examples. It brings to the reader useful condensation of a huge library of writings. For example, page 163 explains how one National Cooperative Research Act of 1984 opens the door to cooperation and to better compatitive position of American industry, now no longer hampered by the stupidity of the Clayton Act, which effectively prohibited cooperation.

It is a pleasure to commend this book to anyone that has an interest in industry, education, or government.

W. Edwards Deming

Washington
26 June 1991

x

Preface

In my previous book, I explained my **understanding** of the Deming Philosophy in terms that made sense to me. Apparently they made sense to a number of other people as well. Again, in this book, I will explain, in terms that make sense to me, how to **operationalize** the Deming Philosophy in business, government, and academia.

This book is divided into two sections. The first is a review of the understanding; the second is a view of the operationalizing.

Section One
Understanding the Deming Philosophy ...
Revolution in Thought
Section Two
Operationalizing the Deming Philosophy ...
Evolution in Practice

Dr. Deming says that you will understand Day 1 of his seminar better after you have finished Day 4. This book is the same. One element of his philosophy (or my approach to operationalize it) is related to many other elements. You will understand Chapter 1 better after you have finished Chapter 6.

I have improved my **understanding** of the Deming Philosophy, as well as how to **operationalize** it, in my position as Director of Total Quality Planning and Statistical Methods for Ford Motor Company, and as a Group Director for General Motors Corporation. I have learned that success does not depend on genius or energy alone, but on the extent to which people have been prepared by what has gone before. In my work I have had the opportunity to learn from some great people (no, they are not rank ordered): Donald Petersen, James Bakken, Donald Ephlin, Robert Stempel, Beverly Bentley, Tom Curry, Dave Travis, William Hoglund, Anne Evans, Laura Busse, Louis Ross, John Katona, Fredrick Herr, Charley Lorber, Joe Bransky, Arvin Mueller, Mike Gracey, Edward Baker, Robert Dorn, Jim Fitzpatrick, Gipsie Ranney, Norbert Keller, Doug Katko, David Chambers, Charlie Best, Gary Cowger, Judy Walker, Vincent Barabba, Peter Jessup, Martha Beard, Richard Brown, Ted Marshall, Rich Monteville, Bill Craft, Harry Artinian, Frank Murdock, Rick Lyons, Scott Rezabek, Bill Capshaw, Victor Kane, Doug Berg, Richard Donnelly, Narendra Sheth, Tom Weekley, Howard Kisner, Bob Farley, Jim Carson, Darwin Foster, Bill Harral, Lonnie Vance, Gordon Brown, Mimi Ritter, Len Brown, Terry Fleming, Larry Moore, Bob Clark, Al Murray, and others of the Crowd and the Quality Network Steering Committee at General Motors, and the Statistical Methods Council and the Total Quality Excellence Steering Committee at Ford.

The one constancy in both of these assignments is my association with Dr. W. Edwards Deming, my teacher and friend. I stated in *The Deming Route to Quality and Productivity: Road Maps and Roadblocks* that I am working to have Dr. Deming known for turning America around, not just Japan. Both of these great companies are much the better because their journey included Dr. W. Edwards Deming.

SECTION ONE

UNDERSTANDING THE DEMING PHILOSOPHY ... REVOLUTION IN THOUGHT

Understanding
The Deming Philosophy...
Revolution in Thought

A few years ago, I understood the overall message of Dr. Deming to be the reduction of waste. My understanding was based upon the many one-sentence descriptors which said "Eliminate" this or "Remove" that. But as you know if you have read my previous book, *The Deming Route to Quality and Productivity: Road Maps and Roadblocks*, the lack of a negative does not connote a strong positive.

Today, I see the aim of his philosophy to be one of balance: balance between the reduction of waste and the addition of value. But the reduction of waste does not insure value. They are not reciprocals.

I also see that his philosophy calls for balance between constancy of purpose and continual improvement; between quantum-leap-innovation and Kaizen-like improvement. His views on optimization span both space and time. There must be balance between the individual and the team, and between short-term and long-term results. Both inputs and outputs are important. Similarly, and in keeping with Confucian teaching, there should be a balance between knowledge and action. A major contribution is the balance of science and philosophy. He brings them back together —from whence they came. And they are both better for it.

If one sentence could summarize or describe the Deming philosophy, I think it would be:

Joy of ownership through joy of workmanship.

The aim of this section is to help you understand the intended impact of that sentence.

Chapter 1

The Processes of
Today's World

One of my biggest frustrations, as I help others improve, is the difficulty I have in getting them to recognize that everything they do can be described in terms of a process. This is not a trivial matter because if one does not believe that everything he does is a process, then he might not be compelled to learn more about how to better manage that process. Every expert and "guru" on Quality are in agreement that processes are everywhere. In spite of this, or maybe because of it, most people in business regard processes as only applicable to manufacturing—and high-volume manufacturing at that. They certainly do not think that processes apply to clerical work, much less to management work. Or do they apply?

NEW YORK (AP) - Prudential Insurance Co. of America stands to lose nearly $93 million if a court rules against it in a case involving three zeroes accidentally dropped from a financial docu-

ment. Prudential says it should not be made to
suffer for a clerical error in a bankruptcy case that
turned its $93 million lien on eight ships into an
insignificant $93,000... Prudential contends that
the mistake is a trivial clerical error. But unse-
cured creditors say that law demands that a vessel's documents be taken at face value...[1]

A huge bank in Chicago ran adrift on to rocky
shores. This trouble would still have occurred
even if every calculation and every piece of paper
handled by the bank had been free of error.[2]

Processes apply not only to manufacturing, but
in the management of every size and shape of organization. In fact, *most* of the opportunities for improvement are in non-manufacturing processes. Dr. Deming
estimates that in the United States, 86 people in 100
are engaged in non-manufacturing or service processes.[3]

In the early 1980's, at Ford, I argued with financial and purchasing and computer people who categori-
cally stated that they managed "systems" not "processes." No amount of logic could convince them otherwise. So we compromised: we used both words. Even
today, I believe, Ford does not use the word "process"
by itself, but rather the term "process/system." The

---

[1] *The Detroit News*, 2 August 1987.
[2] W. Edwards Deming, *Out of the Crisis* (Cambridge: MIT CAES, 1986).
[3]Ibid.

need for the extra word defies logic, but as Nobel Laureate Percy Bridgman stated, "a proof presented to me with the authority of the greatest logician in the world is not a proof to me unless I can 'see' it."[4] I will attempt to shed light on the term "process" from a number of different perspectives so that you may better "see it."

Definition of Process

What is this process that many people find so difficult to understand? It is virtually everything you do and everything you think. Whether you manage a company or manage to get by, plan an attack or plan a party, do a pilot study or do lunch, check a mistake or check out, act on impulse or act your age, write a check or write a book, drive to work or drive a golf ball, conduct a meeting or conduct an orchestra, make a decision or make a sandwich, assemble a satellite or assemble a crowd, you do it through a process.

In its simplest form, a process is a transformation of inputs into outputs (see Figure 1.1). There are five generic resources that are both inputs and outputs:

- People
- Method
- Material
- Equipment
- Environment

---

[4] Percy Bridgman, *Reflections of a Physicist*, (New York: Philosophical Library, 1955).

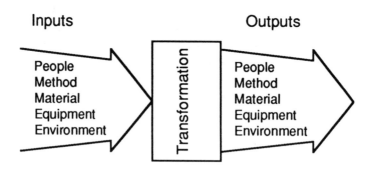

Figure 1.1
Definition of a Process

You should not simplistically focus on **Material** as the process output. All resources transform, or change their state, over time. For instance, as I write this book, I (People) grow tired. I realize that I must review (Method) this manuscript with Dr. Deming more than I had planned. Blank paper (Material) goes into the printer and a masterpiece comes out! My Macintosh Laserwriter (Equipment) gets a little closer to the time that its cartridge must be replaced. Anxiety (Environment) creeps in as I realize how much I have yet to write.

Some inputs and outputs (depending on your perspective) of processes that should be of interest to many managers include those in the following list.

- ROA, ROE, ROI
- Revenues, Costs, Profits
- Cash flow, Line of credit
- Market share, Units of production
- Inventory turns, Inventory value
- Attendance, Absenteeism, Morale
- Things-Gone-Wrong, Things-Gone-Right
- Engineering changes, Patents per R&D $
- Deteriorating and Improving processes
- Straight-time hours, Overtime hours
- Accidents, Wellness
- Visits to customers, Visits to suppliers
- Policies, Directives, Suggestions
- Delighted customers, Complaints
- Delighted employees, Grievances

There are downstream customers for each of these outputs, just as there are upstream suppliers for each of the inputs (Figure 1.2). When I use the term *customer* and *supplier*, I mean the succeeding and preceding process, respectively.

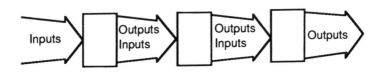

Figure 1.2
Customer-Supplier Relationships

A customer, or for that matter a supplier, does not have to be a person. It could be the next machine receiving the output material. It could be the institution which receives a report or procedure. It may be the environment, which receives the effluents. It could take the form of any of the resources: People, Method, Material, Equipment, or Environment.[5] The outputs of any organization are the result of an interdependent network of processes. If you took away all of the organizational, geographical, and functional boundaries that management has created, you would be left with a process flow which I call the "micro-transactions" of an organization (see Figure 1.3).

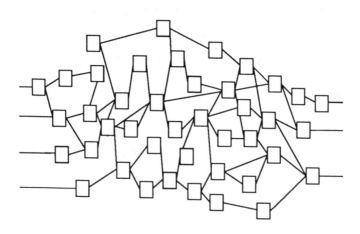

Figure 1.3
Interdependent Network of Processes

[5]William W. Scherkenbach, *The Deming Route to Quality and Productivity: Road Maps and Roadblocks* (Washington: CEE-Press, 1986).

This is the "informal organization," or the way the work gets done. There could be any and every combination of vertical, horizontal, and diagonal customer and supplier transactions, as seen in Figure 1.3. Real organizations cannot, and should not, be described by the neat and orderly columns and rows, as graphically described by many of the organization charts that are seen in companies everywhere. (Or, as Bertrand Russell said, "... any of the other properties that governesses love.")[6]

If you look (with careful attention to detail) at the process model in Figure 1.4, you see that these customer and supplier transactions are facilitated by two sources of communication:

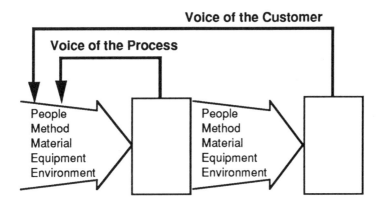

Figure 1.4
The Two Voices

---

[6] Bertrand Russell, *The Scientific Outlook* (New York: W.W. Norton and Company, 1931).

One voice is from the customer, and the other is from within the process itself. I call these the **Voice of the Customer** and the **Voice of the Process.** Like any voice, they can be active or passive.

The **Voice of the Customer** communicates to you the producer, the wants and needs of your customers, as you perceive them. It can also be more generally viewed as the forecast, goal, plan, aim, prediction, objective, target, "druthers," or as Dr. Deming sometimes says, "fact-of-life." Dr. Deming also points out that the generic term *customer* includes all forms of non-customers, such as someone else's customer or a potential customer who is not now in the market. As you shall see later, it also incorporates a number of other *Voices*, from the assembler, to the manufacturer, to the designer, to the banker, to the inventor, or to other experts in subject matter. If you listen to only a single voice, you do so with incalculable risk.

Peter Drucker tells about the German chemist who developed Novocaine as the first local anesthetic. Unfortunately, the doctors refused to use it; they preferred general anesthesia. Quite unexpectedly, dentists began using it, whereupon, the chemist began making speeches against Novocaine's use in dentistry. After all, he had not designed it for that purpose![7]

Dr. Deming tells us that the customer is the most important part of the production line. Aristotle thought so too:

---

[7]Peter F. Drucker, *Innovation and Entrepreneurship* (London: HarperCollins, 1986).

... the user or the master of a house will be a better judge of it than the builder; ... and the guest will be a better judge of a feast than the cook.[8]

The Voice of the Customer can be translated, or operationally defined, in a variety of ways. You know it as the familiar target, and the familiar, but misleading, "goal-posts." You sometimes recognize it as the more useful, but little known, parabola (Figure 1.5). (Chapter 5 discusses the parabolic loss function.)

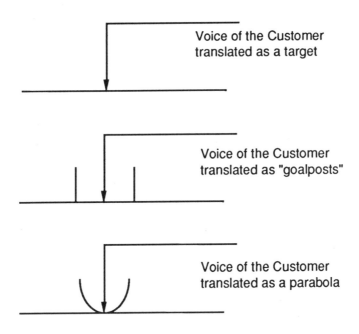

Figure 1.5
Three Expressions of the Voice of the Customer

[8]Aristotle, *Politics*, trans. H. Rackham (Cambridge: Harvard University Press, 1944).

The Voice of the Customer serves to characterize and give dimension to the process inputs and outputs that were introduced in Figure 1.1. They are not just engineering tolerances. They could be a range of salaries, a window of time for the delivery of a proposal; or a high and low estimate of the amount of money needed for a year of college. They could also include a budget estimate for inventory turns in a year, a forecast of sales for the month, a design point for stoichiometry, or a time-phased cash flow plan. Managers might see them as an estimate of the number of delighted customers, a prediction of a change in market share, or a forecast of the amount of time needed to effectively coach and counsel the employees in their care.

The **Voice of the Process** is the *actual* output, or what Dr. Deming describes as the *result* the process gives you. It also can be translated in different ways. Its translation, like the Voice of the Customer, is heavily dependent on the sampling method that you choose.

The job of every person who is in the role of a process manager is to **match** the Voice of the Customer with the Voice of the Process.

You will note that in Figure 1.6, both voices moved, in order to be matched. The Voice of the Customer can be moved through advertisement, a chat with your customer in the next office or operation, by customers talking with other customers, or by some other influence on customers. The Voice of the Process can be moved through the adjustment of People, Material, Method, Equipment, and Environment.

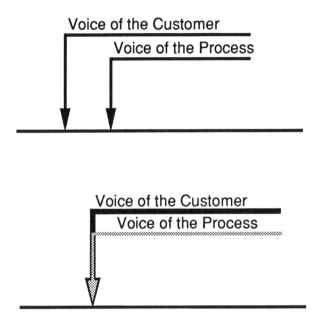

Figure 1.6
Aligning the Voices

In a deterministic world, or one that does not admit to or understand variation, if the *actual* (Voice of the Process) does not match the *plan* (Voice of the Customer), you are asked to explain what happened. It is common in business to "explain all variances."

In Figure 1.7, the February forecast of units to be sold in the month of March was shown to be 20,000. But the actual number of units sold in March was only 18,000. The variance is 2,000 units on the low side. What happened? What is the problem? Why were

2,000 units not sold? What are you going to do to make sure that it does not happen again? How are you going to make up the 2,000 units?

These questions are probably familiar to many of you. And you shall see that they are in need of drastic change because they greatly contribute to waste.

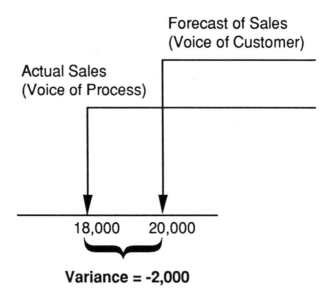

Figure 1.7
The Difference Between the Voices

Variances should not come as a surprise. Some days are better than others when it comes to any of the characteristics listed on page 9. Sales do go up and down every month, absenteeism changes daily, ROI fluctuates for each project, the number of overtime hours varies by plant. One may experience the gamut of emotions, from joy to fear, within a day's work. We live in a world filled with variability—and yet, there is very little recognition or understanding of variability.

The late Professor David Chambers often used this cartoon to emphasize the fact that although variability is commonplace in our life, we are surprised when it happens in our formal places of work.

"I think they all popped at once."

The Popcorn Cartoon
From the work of David S. Chambers
(Cartoonist Unknown)

We do not expect the popcorn to pop all at once! In fact, we understand and even expect that the individual kernels will pop at different times. Why should we be surprised that our businesses perform in a similar fashion?

As shown in Figure 1.8, Management thinks that if only their **People** did as they were told (**Methods**), used the expensive **Equipment** they were provided, used the **Materials** (that were bought at the lowest price), and worked in the participative **Environment** which was installed last month, then all of the output would be the same.

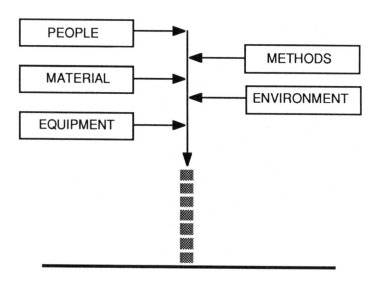

Figure 1.8
Naive View of a Process

You know that in spite of these wishes and hopes, the output will not all be the same.

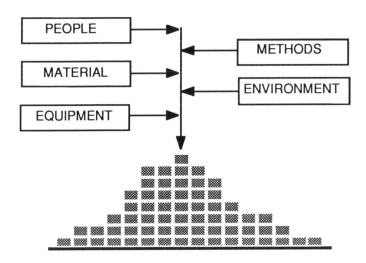

Figure 1.9
The Way Processes Actually Behave

Variability occurs in both the Voice of the Customer and the Voice of the Process. You can see variability in the Voice of the Customer because not all customers buy (or even prefer) the same type of motor vehicle. They have different opinions on any specific model and all of those opinions vary with time. If those variations are predictable over time, or in other words stable, you may look at them as a distribution which may or may not indicate niche markets or special groupings of opinions, depending on its shape.

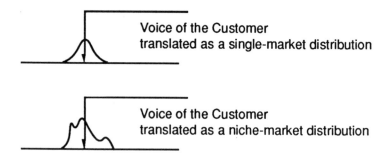

Figure 1.10
Two Expressions of the Voice of the Customer

From the **Voice of the Customer**, you can detect variability in forecasts, if you look at them over time in run chart form, or collapsed over time in histogram form (see Figures 1.11 and 1.12).

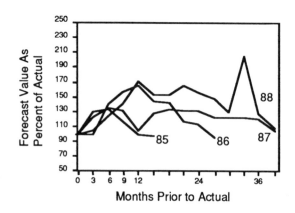

Figure 1.11
The Voice of the Customer in Run Chart Form

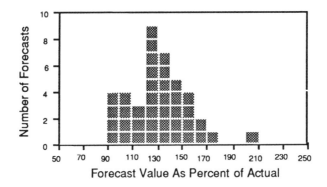

Figure 1.12
The Voice of the Customer in Histogram Form

In Figure 1.13, the **Voice of the Process,** is shown by the variability in the number of "no-shows" for scheduled airline flights. That there is variability in the ages of top executives, is also demonstrated in Figure 1.13. These Voice of the Process histograms can display varying shapes, central tendencies, and spreads.

Because variability is not commonly recognized in our formal processes, there is a lack of *usable* methods to *efficiently* manage it. I stress the word "usable" because if the methods are overly complex or obtuse, they will not be used. I stress the word "efficiently" because many of the methods we have employed have been costly and wasteful. They rely on the use of brute force and overly simple assumptions to "control" and "cajole" the variability—or at least to give the appearance of doing so. To fight variability in the organization, managers have added people for mass inspection, audits, or oversight programs—in order to assure a consistent following of their policies and procedures. On the manufacturing floor, they have installed machinery and people who inspect and sort the good from the bad. In the board room, managers have demanded that any variance be reported, explained, and then rectified.

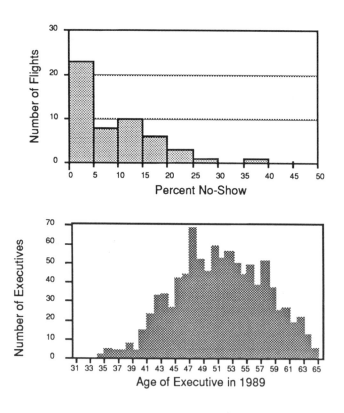

Figure 1.13
The Voice of the Process in Histogram Form

We might have gotten by with these methods when we were competing against ourselves, because they were assumed to be the way to assure quality. But we are in a new economic age. We cannot afford the high cost of "control." We cannot continue to rely on the **Method of Detection of Defects**.

The regulations read:

"The supervisor and compositor shall be flogged thirty times for an error per chapter; the printer shall be flogged thirty times for bad impression, either too dark or too light, of one character per chapter."

(Korean, circa 1450)[9]

The Detection of Defects

The old, expensive method of process management was **The Method of Inspection** (in other words, the output of the Voice of the Process compared to the "goalpost" specification of the Voice of the Customer). This method contained two stages: the first screen passed the *supposedly* good outcomes on to the customer. The second screen, necessary for financial

---

[9]Daniel Boorstin, *The Discoverers: A History of Man's Search to Know His World and Himself* (New York: Vintage Books Division of Random House, 1985).

reasons, reinspected the *supposedly* bad outcomes to determine which might be reworked and returned to the revenue stream. The rest was scrapped or offered as "seconds."

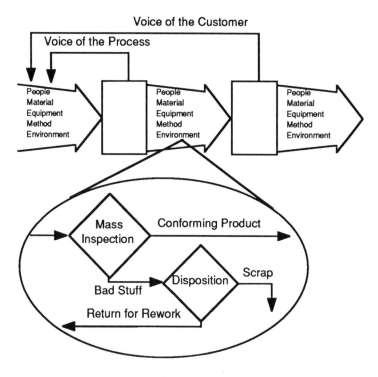

Figure 1.14
The Detection of Defects

I use the term "supposedly" because of the variability of the inspection process itself. We commonly mistake good for bad and bad for good, or otherwise misclassify the outcomes, even with the most careful inspection. This variability is not just restricted to the inspection process; every process has variability.

Dr. Deming often shares the homey story of a little girl who explained how to make toast. Her recipe, which she had learned from her mother, was "First you burn it, then you scrape it." She knew no other way.[10]

The waste of make—inspect—rework ... make—inspect—rework ... is built into many processes because we know of no other way. The waste is everywhere: layer upon layer of managers to inspect and rework the myriad of reports that go up and down the chain-of-command; automated warehouses that inspect and rework each order; all forms of problem-solving; lack of trust; inability to delegate; the use of substitute workers to replace those who are absent; engineering changes. These are but a few examples of waste that we take for granted—because we know of no other way.

---

[10]"The Deming Library," Vol. II, (Chicago: Films Inc.).

The Red Bead Experiment

The red bead experiment is a major highlight in Dr. Deming's 4–day seminar. This simple demonstration makes a number of points that are vital to his philosophy (they are listed in no particular order):

- Quality is made at the top.
- Rigid and precise procedures are not sufficient to produce exact quality.
- People are not always the dominant source of variability.
- Data that are rank ordered can be misleading.
- Keeping the place open with only the *best* workers can set the stage for disappointment.
- Numerical goals are often meaningless.
- Mechanical sampling does not give the same results as sampling with random numbers.
- Picking out the red beads through inspection is a very expensive and inefficient method to eliminate defects.

I will elaborate on each of these points later. First you need to list the resources that make up the red bead process—it should be noted that the necessary materials for this experiment (excluding people!) can be purchased in a pre-assembled kit from a number of sources. To improve a process, it can be helpful to check the resources needed. This can be accomplished with a simple list or a cause-and-effect diagram. One of my own internal consistency checks is the resource categories of the process model:

People: Foreman (Dr. Deming)
6 Willing Workers
Recorder
Chief Inspector
2 Inspectors
Audience

Material: White Beads
Red Beads
Transparencies
Paper

Equipment: Paddle with 50 Beveled
  Depressions
2 Tupperware Boxes
Overhead Projector
Table
Black Transparency Pens

Environment: Indoors, preferably, dominated by a "traditional" foreman.

Method: See flow diagram.

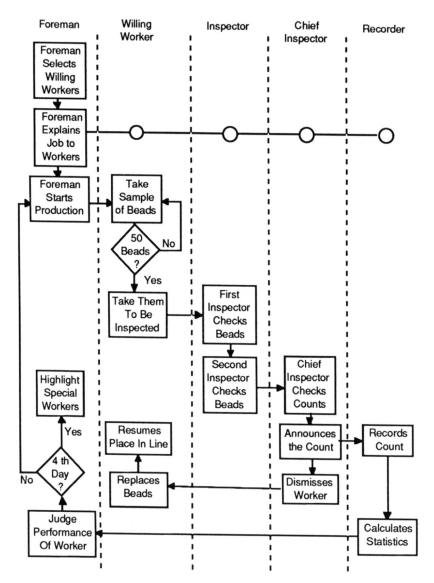

Figure 1.15
Flow Diagram of the Red Bead Experiment

As descriptive as this flow diagram is, you really should *experience* the red bead experiment at a 4–day seminar with Dr. Deming. The next best thing is to watch Dr. Deming on videotape. The red bead experiment tapes are a part of "The Deming Library" videotape series Volumes VII and VIII.[11]

We are now ready to expand on what I think are the important lessons of the red bead experiment.

Quality is made at the top.

The quality of decisions made by the top leaders of a company has a far greater impact on the prosperity of the enterprise than the efforts exerted by the willing workers. The decision to produce white beads in the first place; the decision to purchase beads from a particular supplier; the decision to use fixed procedures; and the decision to rely on mass inspection—all these decisions contributed far more than the willing workers to the waste, the lack of quality, and "going out of business."

Rigid and precise procedures are not sufficient to produce exact quality.

The Foreman made sure that each willing worker followed exactly the procedures he prescribed. But in spite of the fact that the willing workers grasped the smaller vessel by the broad side, let gravity do the

---

[11]"The Deming Library," Vols. VII & VIII, (Chicago: Films Inc.).

work, dipped the paddle into the beads, agitated and then stopped, tilted the paddle 13 degrees and withdrew it from the beads—there were still varying amounts of red beads produced. The distribution of the number of red beads (Voice of the Process) over 35 years worth of experiments looks something like the graph in Figure 1.16.

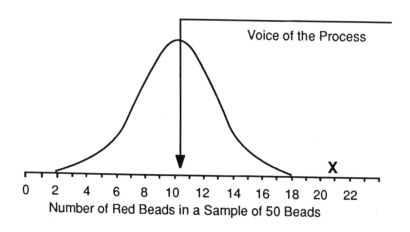

Figure 1.16
The Distribution of Red Beads Over 35 Years

Although the number of red beads drawn over time is predictable within a range of values (in this case from 2 to 18, with one unexplained exception at 21), the exact number of red beads in any one paddle is not predictable.

People are not always the dominant source of variability.

Since the process of the production of red and white beads is predictable, you can determine the contributions that the process resources make to the variability of the outcomes. It is obvious that there will be variability in the number of red beads because there is variability in the process which produced them. Some processes are dominated by People—that is, people contribute the most to the central tendency, shape, and spread of the outcomes. Other processes are dominated by Equipment, Material, Methods, Environment. Still others are dominated by the interactions between these various resources.

In the red bead experiment, Dr. Deming has purposefully eliminated the source of variability that many people think is always the dominant source: that is, the people.

The common wisdom is that if only people did not make so many mistakes, there would not be so many problems. But even with the variability contributed by the people reduced to zero (Figure 1.17), there is still too much variability in the process. There are still too many problems (red beads).

The major contributors to variability in this process are, of course, the beads (Material); the strict mixing procedure and the lack of permission for the willing workers to change the process (Method); even to a small extent, the paddle (Equipment); and to a smaller extent, the indoor environment (Environment).

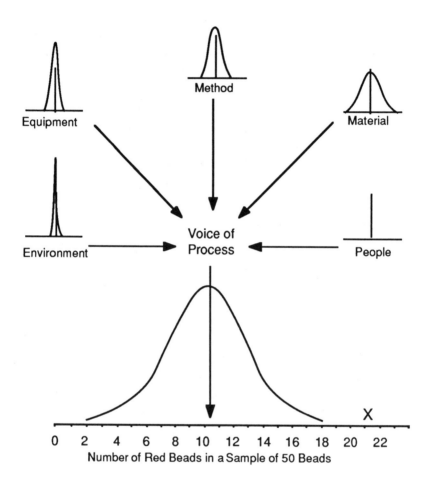

Figure 1.17
Sources of Variation in the Red Bead Experiment

Data that are rank ordered can be misleading.

Regardless of the degree to which People, Material, Method, Equipment, or Environment contribute to the outcomes of a process, their contributions will vary over time. The rank ordering of data implies that different numbers are different from one another. This might seem to be an obvious statement, but it is assuredly not a trivial one.

From the point of view of a one-time customer, all outcomes **can** be rank ordered. Your customers have a right to prefer one number over another. **The scale of measures of desires of customers is absolute.** For customers, each different number or outcome is different. In the red bead experiment, customers have a right to say that 0 red beads are better than 1 red bead, or that 2 red beads are better than 3.

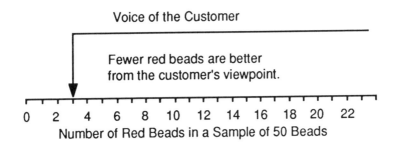

Figure 1.18
The Voice of the Customer is Absolute

You must listen to your customers, but you must also listen to your process. **The scale of measures of the process is relative, not absolute.** Different numbers are *not* necessarily different from each other. They may be the same, from a process point of view.

Dr. Deming's red bead process predictably produces from 2 to 18 red beads per paddle. As Figure 1.19 shows, from the perspective of the red bead process, no meaningful differences are produced. Ten red beads is no different from 18 red beads or from 3. A willing worker might produce 12 red beads one day and 4 the next. (The one-time production of 21 red beads however, was different from the rest. Something special—which Dr. Deming has not yet identified— happened. It was a rare occurrence for this experiment.)

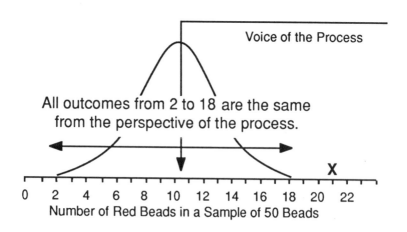

Figure 1.19
The Voice of the Process is Relative

Keeping the place open with only the *best* workers can set the stage for disappointment.

This lesson directly follows from the previous one. If the data show, through the Voice of the Process, that the numbers are all from the same predictable process, then you should not differentiate any of the outcomes that fall within the process limits. At the onset you know that the results of some workers will be above average and some will fall below average. The question a leader must ask is, "What will be their performance in the future?" If the results are all from the same stable process, the answer to the question must be that their performance will fall randomly within the same limits. Just because some were above average in the past does not mean that they will be above average in the future.

Numerical goals are often meaningless.

You just saw that the willing workers cannot affect the number of red beads which they produce. Neither can they recommend changes to the process, in an effort to increase the number of white beads going to their customers. Under these conditions, the Voice of the Customer, translated into a goal of 3 red beads or less by the foreman (see Figure 1.20), has no effect on the number of red or white beads produced. In fact, the goal itself—whether it be 0 or 3 or 23—will have no effect on the number of red or white beads produced by this process.

The leadership, just "doing their best," invested in this process. A set of leaders who possessed Profound Knowledge might have invested in a process that would have enabled the willing workers to contribute to the quality of the outcomes (less red, more white) as well as to the improvement of the process.

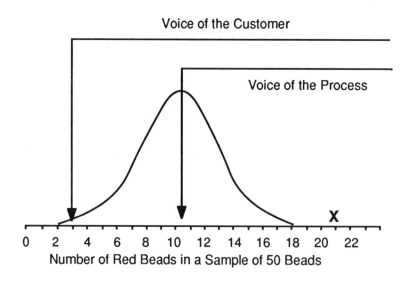

Figure 1.20
The Two Voices for the Red Bead Experiment

Mechanical sampling does not give the same results as sampling with random numbers.

This *seemingly* simple statement is fundamental to the use of statistical methods in the real world. This statement can mean the difference between profit and loss. All *theories*, statistical or otherwise, are correct. The important thing is whether they are useful to you, and statistical methods can only be useful if certain assumptions are fulfilled. If you wish to statistically infer to People, Material, Method, Equipment, or Environment, a description garnered from production samples, you must use random numbers in the sampling method. If you do not use random numbers, your inference is based solely on your perceived knowledge of the subject matter (a theory of knowledge will be elaborated on in Chapter 5).

It is important to remember the difference the paddle makes in the number of red beads drawn. If the beads were numbered and random numbers were used to sample 50 beads from the group of 3750 beads (3000 white and 750 red), the average number of red beads per 50 selected would be 10.[12] But Dr. Deming does not use random numbers. He uses paddles to mechanically scoop out beads from a mechanically mixed group of beads. He has used at least 4 different paddles over the years and each has performed differently. However, none has an accumulated average of 10 red beads.

In the real world, if your break-even point was 10 red beads, and the paddle your workers were using produced an average of 9.2 red beads, you would wonder why no profit was being made. The reason, of course, is that the paddle you were using was telling you that things were better than they really were. If you used random numbers or a different paddle, the

---

[12] W. Edwards Deming, *Out of the Crisis* (Cambridge: MIT CAES, 1986), p. 346.

message would be different. We are beyond the days when we could say that 9.2 is "close enough" to 10—so why worry about it! We are in a new economic age; one that is very competitive.

Picking out the red beads through inspection is a very expensive and inefficient method to eliminate defects.

Dr. Deming's question to the participants is whether or not the number of red beads in each paddle can be decreased—and if so, how? Typically there are several suggestions, ranging from picking them out of the paddle after they are drawn, to picking them out of the box before the 50 beads are drawn. All of the suggestions are forms of "scraping burnt toast." Some people also suggest working with the supplier of beads to increase the number of white beads. But if the supplier does the sorting, that is only another form of "scraping the burnt toast." *But there is a better way.*

13

---

[13]"Willy 'N Ethel," Joe Martin, North America Syndicate, Inc.

The Prevention of Defects

The Method of Prevention of Defects is a different way to manage a process. It can be a better way to manage because it is less costly than the Method of Detection of Defects. The aim of the Method of Prevention of Defects is to preclude bad outcomes from occurring in future process runs.

Before it move, hold it,
Before it go wrong, mould it,
Drain off water in winter before it freeze,
Before weeds grow, sow them to the breeze.
You can deal with what has not happened,
can foresee
Harmful events and not allow them to be.

Laotzu (circa 600 BC)[14]

The use of statistical methods (as shown in Figure 1.21) is the key to the prevention of the bad outcomes. Remember that from the perspective of a customer, all variation is the same: it is bad. You know that the customer has a right to prefer one or several outcomes to others, and that any variation from those preferences is not appreciated.

---

[14] Laotzu, *The Way of Life*, trans. Witter Bynner (New York: Perigee Books, 1944).

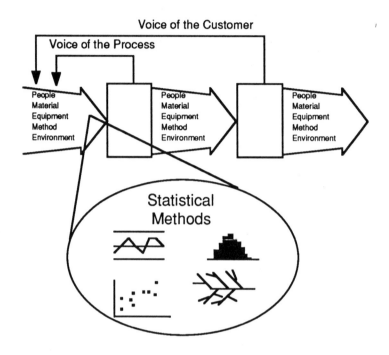

Figure 1.21
The Prevention of Defects

If you viewed the world as deterministic, you would probably adjust or reblend your resources when you realized that the current blend had created problems. That would be a perfectly rational approach—if the world was deterministic in nature. But you saw earlier that this world is not deterministic, but rather, it is variable. In a variable world, if you treat all problems as something special, or something actionable, you will often only make them worse by your tampering. You need to understand more about variability than how to make popcorn if you are to change the process to preclude future defects—without the high cost of detection or the high cost of tampering.

The Funnel Experiment

At each of his 4–day seminars, Dr. Deming conducts the "Nelson Funnel Experiment."[15] This procedure is a very powerful lesson on a common-sense (but flawed) way to prevent defects. It is a simple experiment, but it makes two points, both of which are *vital* to the philosophy of Dr. Deming:

- There are many processes where the people can and do affect the outcomes.

- Chaos can occur when those people use inappropriate methods to try to affect the outcomes. (Dr. Deming calls this tampering.)

The resources needed for the Nelson Funnel Experiment include the following (trainers may wish to note that all of these materials—except the people—are available in a pre-assembled kit):

---

[15] W. Edwards Deming, *Out of the Crisis* (Cambridge: MIT CAES, 1986), p. 327.

People:	Anyone
Material:	Marble
	Tablecloth
Equipment:	Funnel
	Holder for the Funnel
	Table
	Water-soluble Pen
Environment:	Preferably indoors and,
	With Joy
Method:	The flow diagram in Figure 1.22 shows the influence of the scientific method (to be further developed in Chapter 2).

Like the red bead experiment, the funnel experiment is part of "The Deming Library" videotape series. It is conducted and explained in Volume IX.[16] In addition, Tom and Eileen Boardman wrote a very good article on the funnel experiment which appears in the December 1990 issue of *Quality Progress*.[17]

---

[16] "The Deming Library," Vol. IX, (Chicago: Films Inc.).

[17] Thomas J. and Eileen C. Boardman, "Don't Touch That Funnel!," *Quality Progress*, December 1990.

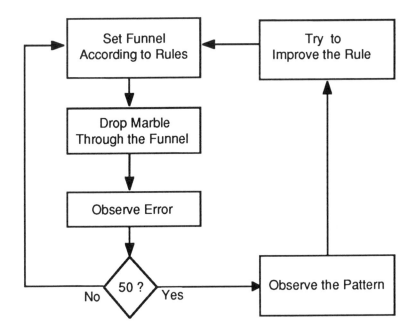

Figure 1.22
Process Flow Diagram for the Funnel Experiment

Rule 1. Leave the funnel fixed, aimed at the target: no adjustment.

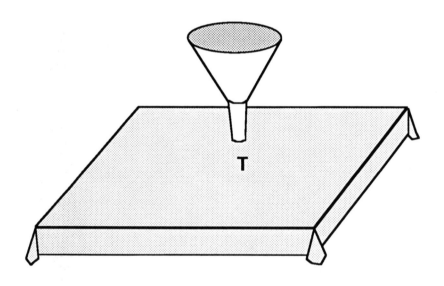

Figure 1.23
Funnel in Position for Rule 1

The aim of this rule is to hit the target. In other words, match the Voice of the Process (marble dropped through the funnel) with the Voice of the Customer (target marked on the tablecloth). The result is a stable distribution of points, only some of which hit the target. The results of the use of Rule 1 are shown in Figure 1.24. As difficult as it is to know when and how to adjust the process to prevent defects, it is even more difficult to know how to improve the process when you have a stable, predictable process and are still producing defects. As good as Rule 1 is, you must do better.

Figure 1.24
Computer Simulation of Rule 1

If you try to improve the process by the use of Rules 2, 3, or 4, even though they are very commonly used, you will not achieve your aim. These rules will only make the results worse. (A method that will lead to improvement on Rule 1 is the subject of Chapter 2.)

Rule 2. After each drop, move the funnel, from its last position, to a point equal to in distance but opposite in direction from the last error. (See Figures 1.25 and 1.26).

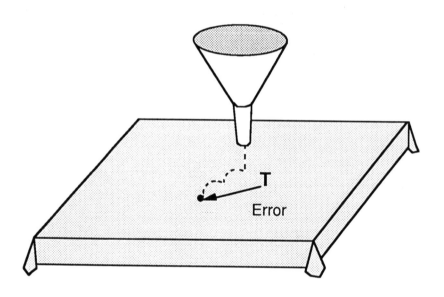

Figure 1.25
Rule 2 for the Funnel

The error is the distance and direction from the target to the place where the marble landed. In Rule 2, it is critical to remember the last position of the funnel because it is the starting point for the new position.

The aim of this rule is to compensate, or move the funnel, so that the next marble is dropped right on the target. Sounds logical, but the result is a stable distribution of points with a spread that is 41 percent greater than (worse than) that obtained by Rule 1 (see Figure 1.27).

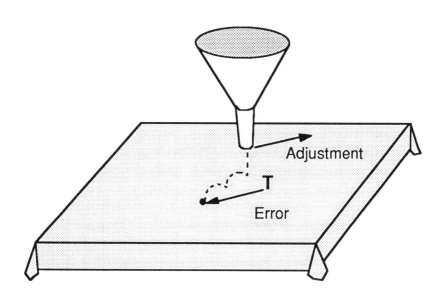

Figure 1.26
Rule 2 for the Funnel

Figure 1.27
Computer Simulation of Rule 2

The automatic compensation device mentioned in *The Deming Route to Quality and Productivity: Road Maps and Roadblocks*[18] followed Rule 2; the calibration of an instrument to a standard can do likewise. You may increase the spread of the measurements if you adjust the instruments or machines every time you compare them to a standard and find they do not match. A color, a dimension, a weight, or any other sensory measure could be a standard. A benchmark, or financial process, or personnel procedure, or value statement could also qualify as a standard.

If you were to make repeated measurements of a standard and did not adjust, or change, or move anything in the process (People, Method, Material, Equipment, or Environment), you would very likely get a predictable distribution of measurements. Some would be above the standard, some below—but the distribution would be predictable.

---

[18] William W. Scherkenbach, *The Deming Route to Quality and Productivity: Road Maps and Roadblocks* (Washington: CEE-Press, 1986).

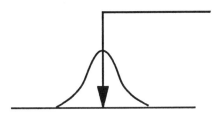

Figure 1.28
Distribution of Measurements of a Standard

You should not consider adjusting to the standard unless the measurement falls outside the limits of the predictable distribution. (You also might adjust the instrument if special patterns of measurements appeared over time.) However, if you adjust the instrument or equipment to a measurement *within* the predictable limits of the distribution of measurements, it will make the variation worse. You would then be "tampering."

I explained this in *The Deming Route*[19] but it bears repeating. If you were to get a measurement on the far right hand side of the predictable distribution of measurements (see Figure 1.29), according to Rule 2, you would adjust the instrument or equipment (funnel) from the center (where the funnel was located) to the far left hand side so that the next measurement would be right on the standard (see Figure 1.30).

[19]William W. Scherkenbach, *The Deming Route to Quality and Productivity: Road Maps and Roadblocks* (Washington: CEE-Press, 1986), p. 33.

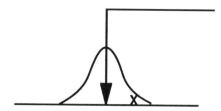

Figure 1.29
Distribution of Measurements of a Standard

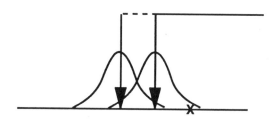

Figure 1.30
Widened Distribution of Measurements of a Standard

You can see that you have increased the variability of the measurement process by this adjustment. And if you followed the logic to its limits, you would widen the limits of variability of measurements by 41 percent over that generated by no adjustment.

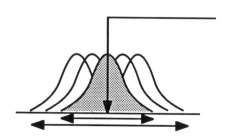

Figure 1.31
Spread of Distribution of Measurements Widened by 41%

Rule 3. After each drop, move the funnel to a point equal to in distance but opposite in direction from the last error (see Figures 1.32 and 1.33)

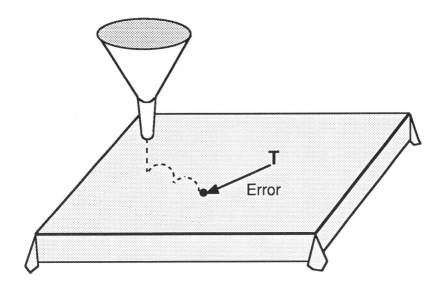

Figure 1.32
Rule 3 for the Funnel

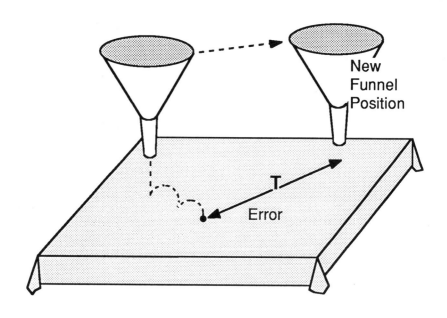

Figure 1.33
Rule 3 for the Funnel

The error is always measured from the target. Flip the error around and you have the new funnel position, regardless of where the funnel was before.

Like Rule 2, the aim of Rule 3 is to compensate the position of the funnel so that the next marble drops right on the target. Unlike Rule 2, the result is an unstable process, which if left to its own devices, explodes, or as Dr. Deming says, goes off to the Milky Way in two directions.

Figure 1.34
Computer Simulation of Rule 3

Two people trying to steady a sailboat by leaning outboard on opposite sides of the craft can cause it to capsize by their alternating efforts. The application of reverse psychology often backfires and results in the opposite of what was intended. For instance, what could seem more reasonable than to try to cheer a person who is depressed? But all too frequently, the depressed person does not benefit from this kind of attention, but sinks deeper into gloom. This prompts others to increase their efforts to make him see the silver lining in every cloud. And so it goes.[20]

---

[20] Watzlawick, Weakland, and Fisch, *Change* (New York: W.W. Norton & Company, 1974).

In the workplace, all forms of expediting only result in ever increasing waiting time, the need for further expediting and further chaos in schedule. And another vicious circle is maintained.

A more personal example involves your attempts to get just the right temperature in the shower. If it is too cold, you might turn up the hot water. This, of course, might then cause you to turn up the cold water. Or, you could turn down the hot water, which might create the need to turn down the cold water as well. And so it goes.

Some people are confused with the difference between Rule 2 and Rule 3. In fact, the first two drops of Rule 3 are the same as Rule 2 because the initial position of the funnel is directly over the target. The main difference is that in Rule 3, the funnel is oscillated back and forth across the Target, regardless of where it has been. But in Rule 2, the funnel movement is based on its last position.

Rule 4. After each drop, move the funnel to a point over the last drop.

Unlike Rules 2 and 3, the aim of this rule is to make all drops the same. You have given up on the Target. But like Rule 3 the result is an unstable process, which if left to its own devices, will wander off to the Milky Way.

Figure 1.35
Computer Simulation of Rule 4

Workers training workers and executives training executives; adjustment of schedules based upon the demands of the last job; a change of company policy based upon the latest attitude survey; engineering changes based upon the last version of the design (without review of the original purpose); the use of the last piece or last batch as the model for the next piece or batch; the tendency to hire people just like yourself (and they, of course, tending to do likewise)—all these practices result in further departures from the intended target.

There are several experiments or exercises which might be used to reinforce the astounding effects of Rule 4. One that I use with the working groups at a 4–day seminar is "The Copy Experiment."

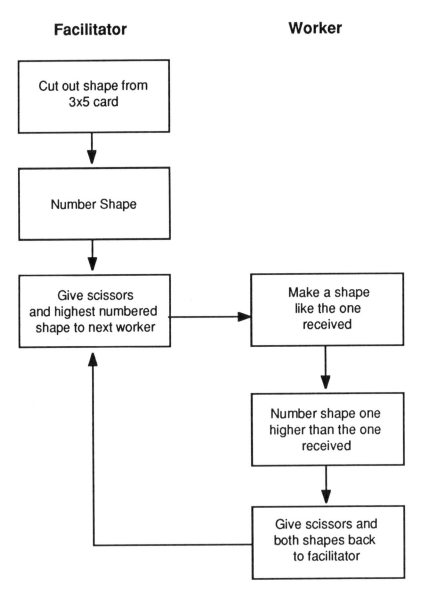

Figure 1.36
Flow Chart of the Copy Experiment

The resources needed for the Copy Experiment are listed below:

People:	At least 50 workers, A facilitator.
Material:	Scissors plus anything that a person has with him.
Environment:	Preferably indoors and with a sense of urgency.
Method:	Follow the flow chart.

I start with simple irregular shapes and by the 50th copy of a copy of a copy, the difference is startling. This is not a new discovery. Daniel Boorstin writes about the effects of copying from copies of Dioscorides' manuscripts for a thousand years. "The copies of copies grew imaginary leaves for symmetry, enlarged roots and stems to fill out the rectangular page. Copyists' fancies became conventions."[21]

I see an interrelationship between the Toast recipe example and the Bead, and Funnel experiments. Dr. Deming presents them as separate entities, and of course, each of them stands on its own merits. But if you look at them as a system of experiments, I think you will get more out of them.

---

[21] Daniel J. Boorstin, *The Discoverers: A History of Man's Search to Know His World and Himself* (New York: Vintage Books Division of Random House, 1985), p. 421.

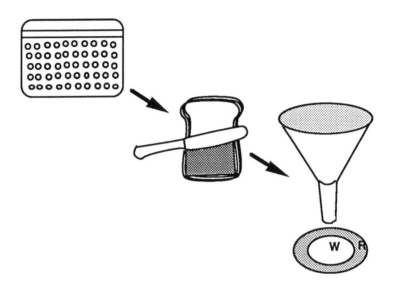

Figure 1.37
The Interrelationships of the Experiments

First, the bead experiment is a lesson on numerical quotas and the difference between common and special causes of variation. Most of the suggestions for the elimination of the red beads are only forms of "scraping the burnt toast." You must go upstream, not to inspect and eliminate red beads, but in order to adjust the process so that red beads will be eliminated.

The funnel experiment can be looked upon as a process whose aim is to make white beads. As long as the beads land within the target area, they are considered to be white. Any that fall outside of the target area are, of course, red. The challenge is to adjust the process in order to make more white beads and less red ones. Some adjustments, namely those that follow Rules 2, 3, and 4, will result in the production of more red beads because more beads will fall outside the target area. Some adjustments, such as painting the outside of the funnel white, will result in no apparent changes. Some adjustments, namely lowering the funnel or wetting the tablecloth, will result in an increase in the number of white beads and a decrease in the number of red beads.

One would like to increase, quick and predictably, the number of white beads. But you know that the logic employed in the funnel experiment will not get you there. For this you need a different logic: you need to understand how to manage a process with use of the **Method of Continual Improvement**.

Chapter 2

The Process of Tomorrow's World: Continual Improvement

Over the years, various experts have proposed numbers of approaches to Problem Solving. You may recognize names such as Kepner-Trego, Alamo, Quality Improvement Process, Team-Oriented Problem Solving, Creative Problem Solving, Analytical Problem Solving, Breakthrough Process, QC Story, and the like. While each has particular strengths, each also has particular weaknesses. All of them have the shortcoming of needing a "problem" to solve. Fortunately, for the problem-solving-industry, there is no shortage of problems! Unfortunately for the rest of us, just solving problems, or reducing waste, or eliminating defects will not make us competitive in this new economic age. We need to go beyond problems and look for opportunities for continual improvement—we must have a new theory.

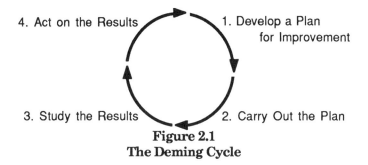

4. Act on the Results   1. Develop a Plan for Improvement

3. Study the Results   2. Carry Out the Plan

Figure 2.1
The Deming Cycle

Robert Reich observed that any product whose requirements can be exactly specified is one destined to be automated, or shipped to a third world country for manufacture. Neither of these choices is necessarily good. The traditional view of value-added work can be shown by taking a pen body, putting on its cap, and then passing it to another station for yet more value-adding. But in the new economic age,

> workers at all levels add value, not by tending machines and carrying out routines, but by continually discovering opportunities for improvement in product and process.[1]

As much as the Method of Prevention was an improvement over the Method of Detection, the **Method of Continual Improvement** is an even greater improvement over both. I do not want to be misinterpreted here, so I will emphasize that the Method of Continual Improvement builds on the good characteristics of both Detection and Prevention. I am not trying to "sell" this method by saying that every other method "gets you nothing." Remember, people are only doing their best. And even the Method of Continual Improvement is itself subject to improvement.

Integral to the Method of Continual Improvement is what the Japanese call the Deming Wheel or Deming Cycle. This Cycle, or the Plan-Do-Study-Act Cycle,[2] might make intuitive sense to many because it is derived from the scientific method. But in order for

---

[1]Robert B. Reich, "Entrepreneurship Reconsidered: The Team as Hero," *Harvard Business Review*, May/June 1987.
[2]This is Dr. Deming's improvement on what most of you know as the Plan-Do-Check-Act.

everyone to be able to use it to improve processes, you must, as Dr. Deming says, operationally define it. I briefly described the Deming Cycle in *The Deming Route to Quality and Productivity*. But my description here and in Chapter 5 goes far beyond any of my earlier works.

We can operationally define the Deming Cycle by setting down a series of 8 action steps. These are general enough for everyone to see their relevance, and specific enough to be followed by any process manager.

I. PLAN:
Develop a Plan to Improve

Step 1:   Identify the opportunity for improvement.

Step 2:   Document the present process.

Step 3:   Create a vision of the improved process.

Step 4:   Define the scope of the improvement effort.

II. DO:
Carry Out the Plan.

Step 5:   Pilot the proposed changes on a small scale, with customers, and over time.

III. STUDY:
Study the Results

Step 6:   Observe what you learned about the improvement of the process.

IV. ACT:
Adjust the Process, based on your new knowledge.

Step 7:   Operationalize the new mix of resources.

Step 8:   Repeat the Steps (Cycle) on the next opportunity.

"Plan" Stage, Step 1:
Identify the Opportunity for Improvement.

This process is accomplished by comparing the "Voice of the Customer" with the "Voice of the Process." Many times these two Voices do not match. This is an opportunity for improvement that I call the Gap (some people know it as capability of a process).

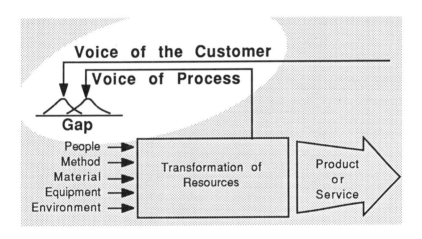

Figure 2.2
The Gap Between the Two Voices

As stated in Chapter 1, both Voices change, or vary, over time. The Gap is not a simple difference of 2 single point values. It incorporates the location, spread, and shape of each voice. The statistical stability of each voice is also critical to your decision on how to reduce the Gap. The process by which each Voice is measured and estimated is also of vital importance. As Dr. Deming reminds us, when you apply a procedure, you get an estimate. If you apply another procedure, you get a different estimate. And in fact, if you apply the same procedure twice, you will get two different estimates.

Example of Step 1.

Timeliness is one of three key characteristics that any process manager should want improved (the other two are quality and cost). The Voice of the Customer, interpreted by management, might say that the developmental lead time for a new automotive vehicle, from its initial Concept to its Commercialization, should be 48 months.

The Voice of the Process, which is the distribution of the actual times taken to deliver a number of new vehicle programs, says that the typical lead time is about 70 months (lowest time being 66 months and highest time being 74 months). The opportunity for improvement is to move the process average down to 48 months, and also to reduce its variability.

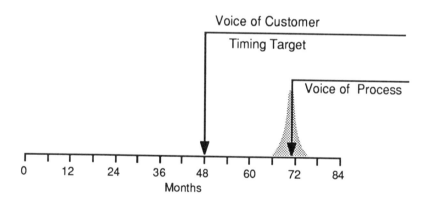

Figure 2.3
Months to Commercialization

In this example, you see that unless you dramatically change the input resources, you will never get the output of the process down to 48 months. It is beyond the capability of the existing process.

"Plan" Stage, Step 2:
Document the Present Process.

The aim of this step is to begin to see the interdependent network of customers and suppliers through the construction of a Process Flow Diagram, or Process Map, as seen in Figure 2.4.

The first time through the Steps, you should construct your view of the process. But the real value is found in the perspectives contributed by other members of your team. There are many ways to construct process flow diagrams. The essential elements in any that you choose to use should include a graphical representation of the customer and supplier interfaces and the relevant linkages of People, Material, Methods, Equipment, and Environment.

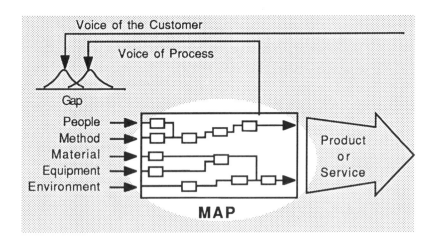

Figure 2.4
Process Flow Diagram

Example of Step 2.

Inland Division of General Motors Corporation wanted to improve the process that they used to set budgets. From the initial budget request from the Corporation, to the submission of the budget from the Division, the process required an average of 190 days. A team of accountants developed a Process Map of the steps in the budget process, as they were best able to discern them. No single accountant was able to generate the agreed-upon Process Map. Every accountant, however, did have an opinion about how it should look. Figure 2.5 is an excerpt of the complex Map that they developed.

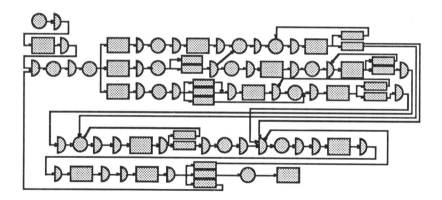

Figure 2.5
Inland's Flow Chart for the Budget Process

Once the existing process is mapped, it is usually relatively easy to identify parts of the process that are redundant, or wasteful, or which could be simplified.

"Plan" Stage, Step 3:
Create a Vision of the Improved Process.

This is similar to the second step. After you have described your perception of the existing process, you must create a vision of the improved process. In other words, you "vision" or "imagineer" or "look at the possibilities" of what the process could look like, given only minimal constraints.

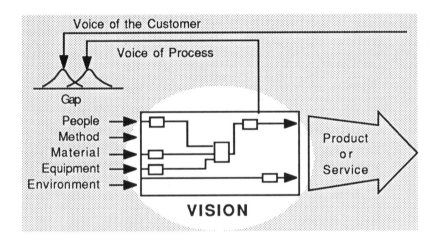

Figure 2.6
Vision of the Improved Process

Steps 2 and 3 are interchangeable. But I find that if I describe the existing process first, especially with complex processes, it helps me to see some of the existing pitfalls and inefficiencies that I probably would have incorporated into the "vision"—because I did not know they existed.

Visioning is not an easy thing to do, because of what Dr. William Ouchi calls superstitious learning. You do many things without question because you have been carefully taught—like the little girl and her toast recipe. The process of developing a vision can be greatly aided by taking the time to operationally define what it is that you think the customer really wants or needs, and to focus on those steps which add value.

Example of Step 3.

After the team of accountants from Inland Division developed the process flow diagram for the budget process, they were able to identify obvious areas of waste (steps that did not add value in the customer's eyes). To improve the process, they proposed some review steps to be done simultaneously instead of serially. They predicted that their revised "vision" would only require an average of 109 days, from start to finish.

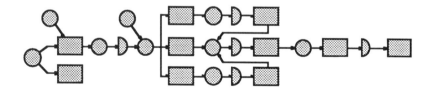

Figure 2.7
Vision of Inland's Improved Budget Process

"Plan" Stage, Step 4:
Define the Scope of the Improvement Effort.

This step must not be attempted until you have cycled through the first three steps, and are ready to define your plan for improvement.

A plan is a statement of intent—a prediction on a future blending of People, Method, Material, Equipment, and Environment. If they are combined in certain ways, the Gap should be narrowed or closed. The plan must ask who, what, when, where, why, how, and how much? In my years at Booz Allen and Hamilton, I learned the importance of key questions for the focus of scarce resources.

The plan must call for the participation of teams of customers and suppliers, as well as individual experts on the subject matter. (For dramatic improvement, include the use of experts in apparently unrelated disciplines.) You must determine the roles and responsibilities of all personnel and what will be postponed or rescheduled to allow time for work on the effort to improve. You must also define the process boundaries, and key characteristics of interest.

Dr. Deming's favorite question is, "By what method will you improve?" Your plan must balance short-term containment and long-term improvement. It must call for the removal of negatives and enhancement of positives. It must carry over learnings from previous cycles and anticipate the focus of future cycles. And it must balance all these factors on three levels: physical, logical, and emotional.

The Plan can take many forms, since people learn in different ways. I prefer to use graphical forms that represent the planned optimization of space and time, as well as all of the other characteristics mentioned above. One such graphical representation is a "Shared Objectives and Interlocking Action Matrix."[2]

---

[2] Jaime Herman and Edward Baker, "Teamwork is Meeting Internal Customer Needs," *Quality Progress*, July 1985.

Example of Step 4.

Ford Division's Order Processing Center had the aim of improving the process of handling vehicle claims from dealers. After a team developed the process flow diagram, they realized that more than just their Division was involved. They had to expand the improvement team in order to get the active participation of all the organizations listed below.

Establishing the Interlocking Actions was important because previously, when the Order Processing Center made efforts to reduce the number of mis-built vehicle claims, the in-transit damage went up, or the zero mileage warranty increased, or the number of mis-invoiced vehicles rose. No unilateral effort had been successful until the team (which included dealers) operationally defined each of those categories and made a visible commitment and a plan to reduce them all.

List of:
Reduce Misbuilt Vehicle Claims

| Ford Parts and Services |
| Dealer Affairs |
| B&AO Controller |
| B&AO Traffic Department |
| Pre-Delivery Service Corp. |
| Lincoln Mercury Division |
| Ford of Canada |
| Order Processing Center |
| Dealer Council |

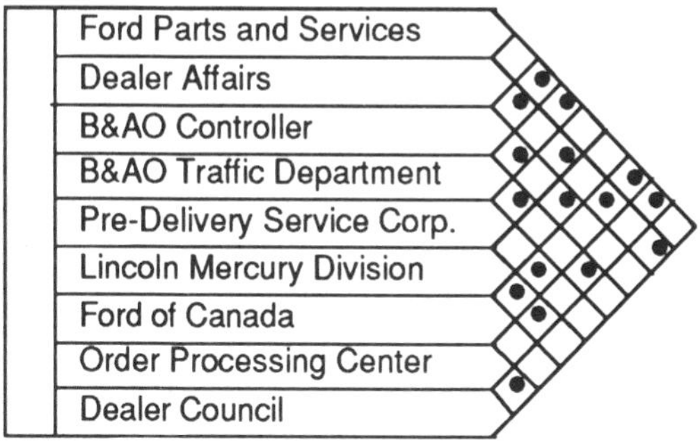

Figure 2.8
Interlocking Action Matrix

"Do" Stage, Step 5:
Pilot the Proposed Changes on a Small Scale,
With Customers, and Over Time.

Some Statistical Thinking can help advance knowledge by making an otherwise costly and paradigm-reinforcing, one-factor-at-a-time experiment more efficient and useful. Design of Experiments is best used by varying many-factors-at-a-time. There are numerous designs available to you: full or fractional factorials; screening designs, such as Taguchi or Plackett and Burman; and accelerated experiments for reliability testing.

It is important for you to know that no matter what the consultants try to sell you, there is no one or single design that is universally useful. The design you choose should have the ability to discover interactions between inputs and/or outputs. This is mandatory if you are to go beyond the "best expert" solutions.

Don't think that experiments are only applicable to hardware or equipment. You might experiment with a change of organization— or Method, or Environment, or People. Were there any unexpected interactions in your plan? They could be positive or negative. If you are to make quantum leaps of improvement, you must be particularly sensitive to positive, synergistic blending of resources where the whole is greater than the sum of its parts—as well as negative, antagonistic blending where the whole is less than the sum of its parts.

If possible, it is important to experiment on a small scale (perhaps a number of small experiments) so as not to put the Company at excessive risk at any one time. It is also important to involve/expose customers in the experiment in order to verify or improve the linkages in the Voice of the Customer.

Example of Step 5.

A Design of Experiments class must decide the "best" alternative design for a paper helicopter. Design characteristics that are critical include: the size of the "rotors" and the amount of ballast on board the craft. The class determined that the duration of flight, measured in seconds, was the response that they would measure to determine the "best" design. In order to examine the effect of rotor size and the amount of ballast on the duration of flight, an experiment was designed, yielding the results in Figure 2.9:

Condition Number	Settings		Duration of Flight
	Rotor	Ballast	
1	2 inch	1 clip	2.51
2	3 inches	2 clips	2.03
3	3 inches	1 clip	2.45
4	2 inch	2 clips	2.05

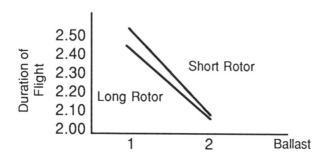

Figure 2.9
A Designed Experiment

Based on the experiment, it appears that the ballast has the greatest effect upon the duration of the flight.

"Study" Stage, Step 6:
Observe What You Learned About
the Improvement of the Process.

The purpose of the experiment was to see if the planned changes in the process would result in a smaller Gap. In other words, you hoped to verify that the capability of the process did improve. Sometimes there is no apparent improvement—other times, the Gap gets worse. And sometimes, the Gap decreases. Whatever the results, we must learn. The Gap might get better because the Voice of the Customer, or the Voice of the Process, or both of them moved. What you learn will depend on the specifics of the movement, not just the change itself.

Statistical Control is a necessary prerequisite for further improvement, because if results are not predictable, you cannot rationally project the outcomes of any process changes that you make.

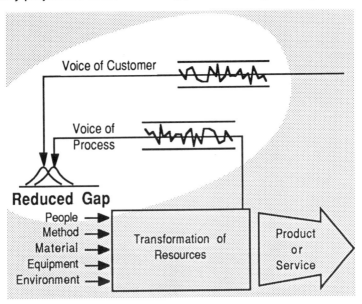

Figure 2.10
Reducing the Gap

Example of Step 6.

An improvement team from Knock-down (KD) Operations in Ford of Europe was established to examine the process of movement of parts from Europe to Venezuela. They piloted the use of colored tags on shipments of parts in an effort to reduce the number missing on arrival in Venezuela. Before the pilot program, the number of missing parts per day ranged from a low of 0 to a high of 6, with an average of 2. After the change, the average number of missing parts per day dropped to less than one-half, with a high of 1.

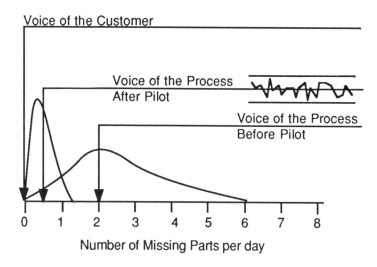

Number of Missing Parts per day

Figure 2.11
Example of Reducing the Gap

During the 2–month pilot, the team kept a control chart of the number of missing parts per day, and it showed that the process was in statistical control. The length of time that the experiment lasted was primarily determined by the amount of time required to give the various resources a chance to vary. The number of points required for statistical reasons was less than the number required by these other concerns.

"Act" Stage, Step 7:
Operationalize the New Mix of Resources Through
Shared Objectives and Interlocking Actions.

This can be reduced to the questions: Who? What? When?
Where? Why? How? How much?

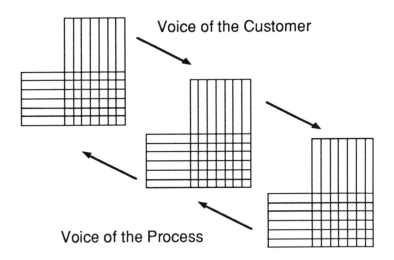

Voice of the Customer

Voice of the Process

Figure 2.12
Deployment of Shared Objectives
and Interlocking Actions

Using the Shared Objectives and Interlocking Actions Matrix that we developed in Step 4, the Improvement Team should first update them to reflect what was learned in the Pilot. Then, they must deploy these between the various levels of Process Managers who were determined to be essential in the operationalization of the improvements.

Example of Step 7.

An Accounts Receivable process in Division A was improved by a team of accountants. Development of the planned improvements for this process required the written agreements of other organizations. For instance, within Division A, a data entry process, which in turn is a part of the Accounts Receivable process, needed improvement. The entire Financial Management Procedure Manual, which encompasses the Accounts Receivable process, also needed revision. The Improvement Team then deployed the objectives and interlocking actions to the appropriate organizations.

The shared objectives and interlocking actions furnished an overall vision of the improved process, the tasks for attainment of the vision, the process for executing these tasks, the resource requirements for each task, the timing for each task, and the key characteristics essential to the achievement of the vision.

"Act" Stage, Step 8:
Repeat the Steps (Cycle) on the Next Opportunity.

As you make permanent the piloted improvement of Step 7, you must determine from where the next iteration of improvement is needed. To do this, you must look at the remaining Gaps in this and other processes. Are there any that are so great in loss that you feel compelled to begin the next cycle there? It may be that further improvement of the same process will have the biggest payoff.

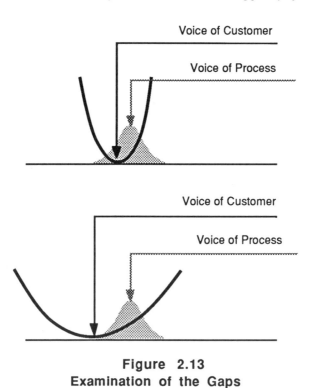

Figure 2.13
Examination of the Gaps

Example of Step 8.

An HVAC system for a lecture hall was improved to hold an average of 71 degrees Fahrenheit within a range of 7 degrees. This made the total cost of the system $ X. The loss the system caused for the customer was $ Y. So the total cost is $ X+Y.

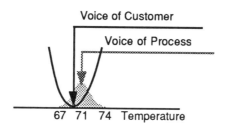

Figure 2.14
The Gap for Lecture Hall Temperature

Other processes which improve a learning environment include the lighting, seating, and acoustics of the lecture hall. You can see that the loss function pertaining to acoustics is far greater than the others, so it could be the focus for the next iteration of the improvement cycle.

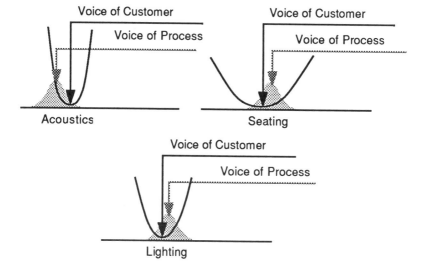

Figure 2.15
Gaps for Other Lecture Hall Characteristics

My view of a process and its improvement is one of similarity at every scale. The model is applicable whether you are improving a macro process as large as the world or a micro process as small as an idea. Different disciplines might use different names for their level of influence, but they all describe the same process. This view is similar to Gleick's popularization of Mandelbrot's work on Chaos.[3]

Whether a method for improvement has 3 or 4 or 5 or 8 or 9 or 29 steps, it should balance science with philosophy. Most methods are typically strong only in one area or the other. The organizational development approaches focus on psychology, while the statistical approaches emphasize science. The improvement of this situation is not as simple as you might expect. You cannot retrofit a philosophy to a science, or vice versa, and expect a truly integrated result. Both must work together in order to make each one better than they could be separately.

As I use these 8 steps for improvement, I rely on my own internal consistency checks at each step. First, I check to see if all the necessary resources are present: People, Material, Method, Equipment, and Environment. Then, each of the resources should be described by some combination of the five senses: Look, Feel, Sound, Smell, and Taste. I then determine if the Physical, Logical, and Emotional levels are included in the plan. Finally, I look for a balance between each person's ability to feel important as an

---

[3]James Gleick, *Chaos Making a New Science* (New York: Penguin, 1987).

individual and also to feel like a part of the team, or family.

The 8–Step Method for Improvement that I outlined in this chapter is a synergistic blend of science and philosophy. The science, or statistics, roots might be more obvious than the philosophy or psychology. In the next chapters, however, I will make the contribution of psychology and philosophy more obvious.

Chapter 3

Some Theory of Change

The aim of the philosophy of Dr. Deming is not just to change, but to change so that there is an improvement over the previous state. But what is an improvement? What is a previous state? What is change? For answers to these questions you must go back many years to the various political, social, and scientific changes that have taken place.

I wanted to refer you to a single book which describes what is covered in this chapter. But after extensive reading and research, I have not found such a volume. And yet, these concepts are not new. They have been the pattern of change for thousands of years in Eastern and Western cultures.

Arthur Schopenhauer wrote that the motto of history should be "Eadem, sed aliter."—the same things, but in different ways,[1]—or the more familiar: the more things change, the more they stay the same.

---

[1]Will Durant, *The Story of Philosophy* (New York: Washington Square Press, 1953).

The Book of Changes (I Ching) has guided Confucianists and Taoists for centuries. Throughout time we have seen changes in People, Materials, Methods, Equipment, and Environments. The same Chinese word is used for both "change" and "easy."[2] How can something which should be easy, be made so difficult by people in today's world?

I believe that many people, if asked how to change something, would respond in terms of their physical environment. You can change the color of a room with a new coat of paint. You can change or replace obsolete equipment with modern technology. You can change jobs. You can make quality a priority by promulgation of a policy. If an organization is not producing as intended, you can change it; you can reorganize. As the folks at Nike say, "Just do it!"

This response is partly based on the assumption that the Second Law of Thermodynamics applies everywhere. It does not. In the inanimate physical world, entropy does increase, and the energy to bring order must come from outside a process. Left unchecked, any physical inanimate process will become less and less organized.[3] But the *living* world has *negative* entropy. Order in living systems is not dependent upon the external sources of energy that organize the inanimate world.

---

[2]Wing-Tsit Chan, *A Source Book in Chinese Philosophy* (Princeton: Princeton University Press, 1963).

[3]L. Leshan and & H. Margenau, *Einstien's Space and Van Gogh's Sky* (New York: Collier Books, 1982).

In the living world, people have more than mere physical dimensions. The development of the human brain has resulted in what amounts to three interconnected structures. Paul MacLean has described our triune brain as being composed of the R-complex, Limbic system, and the Neo-cortex.[4] Each of the three portions of the human brain has specific functions, and each is neurally connected to the others. The focus of the R-complex is to regulate physical bodily functions such as metabolism, digestion, respiration and the like. The focus of the Limbic system is emotional: joy, fear, terror, delight, empathy, and hormonal regulation. The focus of the Neo-cortex is cognitive or logical. The Neo-cortex portion is the largest part of the human brain. It adds expanded memory capacity and refined motor and sensory functions.[5]

If you want to change people, you must seek to affect all three portions of their brains: the physical, the emotional, and the logical. Different people and cultures share many of the same concepts regarding the triune brain, but have used different words, or metaphors, or symbols to represent them. Many of these descriptive words are found in the chart on the following page (each row describes a set of terms).

---

[4]Carl Sagan, *The Dragons of Eden* (New York: Ballantine Books, 1977).

[5]C. Laughlin, J. McManus, and E. d'Aquili, *Brain, Symbol & Experience* (Boston: New Science Library, 1990).

Physical	Logical	Emotional
Hand	Head	Heart
Psychomotor	Cognitive	Affective
Physical	Rational	Spiritual
Government	Academia	Church
Masculine	Rational	Feminine [6]
Position	Knowledge	Charisma [7]
Adaptive	Cognitive	Intuitive
Coercive	Rational	Normative [8]
Financial capital	Intellectual capital	Good will
Skills	Knowledge	Attitude

If you were a Boy Scout, you remember reciting the Scout oath: "... physically strong, mentally awake, morally straight." You were probably not aware of the profundity of those words. With apologies to Robert Fulghum, all you needed to know about change, you learned as a Scout!

---

[6]These are categories of leaders taken from *The Heart of Business*, Peter Koestenbaum (Dallas: Saybrook Publishing Company, 1987).

[7]These are categories of power from "New Ways to Exercise Power," Thomas Stewart. *Fortune Magazine*, 6 November 1989.

[8]Bennis, Benne, & Chin, *The Planning of Change* (New York: Holt, Rinehart and Winston, 1985).

In the East, ("The Great Learning"), Confucius described the place for knowledge, will, and acts:[9] (logical, emotional, and physical). In the West, Plato spoke about the tripartite human nature: appetite, reason, and spirit.[10]

One must realize that in spite of the evolutionary development of the brain—from the R-complex, to the Limbic system, to the Neo-cortex—change in people is not hierarchical. That is, Logical is not more important than Emotional, which is no more important than Physical. Each is necessary, but not itself sufficient, to facilitate the changes needed for continued prosperity in today's new economic age.

I visualize the relationships between physical, logical, and emotional, as an intersecting Venn Diagram (Figure 3.1). There are specific strategies for change that appeal to each—as well as to their intersections. Three intersections are obvious. Psychology is the combination of emotion (soul) and logic. Art is the combination of emotional and physical. Science is the combination of physical and logical. I think that the intersection of all three is, what is called in the east, *harmony*—or what Abraham Maslow called *peak experiences*.[11] It is a balance that differs in each indi-

---

[9]Confucius, *The Analects of Confucius,* trans. Arthur Waley (London: HarperCollins, 1938).

[10]Will Durant, *The Story of Philosophy* (New York: Simon & Schuster, 1953).

[11]Abraham Maslow, *Toward a Psychology of Being* (New York: Van Nostrand Reinhold, 1968).

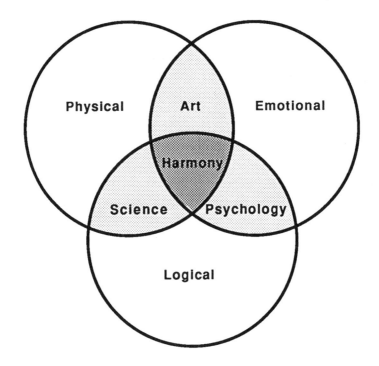

Figure 3.1
The Relationships Between
Physical, Logical, and Emotional Change

vidual, but it results in an output that is greater than the sum of its parts.

While this representation might appear overly simplistic, I think that it effectively makes the point. Each part does not stand alone—there are a number of dynamic interactions and overlaps which can predictably occur and for which methods, or strategies for change, must be developed.

The physical, logical, and emotional categories are another of my own internal consistency checks. Does my plan for change incorporate all of these categories? If not, then it must be revised. Have I incorporated all of the categories as I act on opportunities for improvement? While there is only a brief description of these categories here, in Chapters 4, 5, and 6, I will present more detail on my use of them as I operationalize the philosophy of Dr. Deming.

The **physical category** is often dominant in workers, as well as executives. Many people only need to be told what to do. Others only want to issue commands, or establish policies, and feel assured that conformance will follow. The physical level is composed of *policies, procedures* and *standards*; *case studies*, and *organizational reporting relationships* (whose supposition is that if you report to me, we will get the job done). The physical category also includes *skills, training, measurements*, and *rewards* and *penalties.*

Talking about Quality is not enough. Unless it is encouraged and provided for in policies and procedures; unless it is the focus of organized project teams or simultaneous engineering teams (which should include statisticians, engineers, manufacturing people, accountants, and others); unless there is a reward system (I prefer to call it an investment system) which gives people a chance to improve quality, there is little chance for improvement to happen.

But even plans which focus on the physical category are not in themselves sufficient to guarantee the change of the entire organization. In addition to the *letter* of the law, you must work to define the *spirit* of the law. This is not just a precept of western culture and religion, but eastern as well.

> Lead the people with governmental measures and regulate them by law and punishment, and they will avoid wrong-doing but will have no sense of honor and shame. Lead them with virtue and regulate them by the rules of propriety, and they will have a sense of honor and shame and, moreover, set themselves right.[12]

The **logical category** is important to engineers, scientists, accountants, statisticians, and all rational people. Its premise is that if only people could be logically convinced of the need to change—to improve—they would certainly feel compelled to change, and indeed, would do so. If only people could see how useful, or how easy, or just what the trick is to improve quality, they would beat down the door to find out more about it. Then, they would hasten to make the necessary changes.

I have seen specific situations where an area manager was, with great fanfare, promoted to the position of plant manager because he followed the philosophy. Likewise, a division general manager was promoted to a vice presidency for the same reason. The aim for these publicized promotions was to demonstrate the logic of the new way and to persuade others

---

[12]Confucius, *The Analects of Confucius,* trans. Arthur Whaley (London: HarperCollins, 1938).

to follow in the footsteps of the newly promoted executives. It persuaded some, but didn't budge others. I am reminded of Charles Darwin who wrote:

> Although I am fully convinced of the truth of the views given in this volume, ... I by no means expect to convince experienced naturalists whose minds are stocked with a multitude of facts all viewed, during a long course of years, from a point of view directly opposite to mine. ... But I look with confidence to the future, to young and rising naturalists, who will be able to view both sides of the question with impartiality.[13]

Most of the experts in quality speak of the necessity to understand their message. So naturally their recipe for change stresses **education.** This is vitally necessary, but again, not sufficient in itself for the change that is needed. *Case studies, promotions and demotions* (for the purpose of setting example), and *explanations of rationale* all operate in the logical category. The **profound knowledge** that Dr. Deming espouses is a part of this logical category. But as Shopenhauer said, "Nobody ever convinced anybody on the basis of logic. Even logicians use logic only as a source of income."[14] Pascal also observed that the heart has reasons which the head can never understand.

---

[13]Charles Darwin, *On the Origin of Species* (Cambridge: Harvard University Press, 1964).

[14]Will Durant, *The Story of Philosophy* (New York: Washington Square Press, 1953).

This brings us to the **emotional category**—for many people in business, the most difficult to plan or implement. People in sales and marketing, or on athletic teams, or artists—or people in the profession of organizational development—seem to readily embrace this level. Pride, joy, and delight, as well as fear and anxiety, are all emotions. Our plans must provide ways to operate on this level, tapping into the *intrinsic motivation* which is within each person. To accomplish this, it is important that the organization's constancy of purpose statement (Voice of the Customer) be congruent with the internalized values of the people (Voice of the Process). Also necessary are plans to remove fear and overcome anxiety, and to improve processes in ways that demand, persuade, and inspire people to take more joy in their lives.

I am often asked, "How can we leapfrog our competition in the international market place?" I think the answer lies in the ability to promote, in our *formal processes*, the ability to find joy in our work. People must feel important as individuals, but they must also feel the need to find joy in being a part of a team.

In America, the workplace does not adequately reinforce the concept of teamwork. In Japan, the importance of the individual is not strongly reinforced. The people in both countries fill the missing part of their lives with their *informal processes*.

In America, observation of the magnitude of volunteer work and the active participation in social and athletic events, demonstrate that if people cannot find joy as a part of a team in the workplace, they will go outside to find this joy. (By the same token, in Japan I see people expressing their individuality in informal settings, but again, outside of the workplace.)

The work place can be improved by the creation of processes which balance these two needs: the need for individuality and the need to be part of a team. This will open the way to greater contributions by all. I do not see the people in Japan recognizing, to any great extent, this need for balance between individualism and teamwork, even though Confucius carefully balanced the individual and society. I think he summed up human beings when he said, "By nature, men are alike. Through practice they have become far apart."[15]

Dependence, Independence, Interdependence

I must expand upon the process model described in Chapter 1 so that you can better see the other elements of this theory of change. A process is a transformation of inputs into outputs. One customer's input is another supplier's output.

---

[15]Wing-Tsit Chan, *A Source Book in Chinese Philosophy* (Princeton: Princeton University Press, 1963).

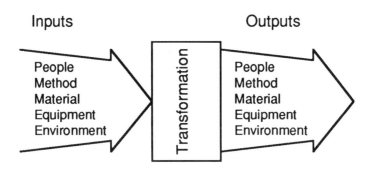

Figure 3.2
Definition of a Process

If you are influenced, controlled, or dominated by either your customer or your supplier, or both, you are in a *dependent relationship*, as shown in Figure 3.3. When you are born, you are completely dependent upon your parents and when you begin school, you are virtually dependent upon your teachers. When you first go to work, you are completely dependent on your boss, or perhaps your co-workers. A company might be completely dependent on its suppliers who may say, "Take it or leave it." An organization could be completely dependent on its customers who sing, "Do it my way."

If you are not influenced or controlled by any customer or supplier, you, the producer, dominate the process. In that case, your process is in an *independent relationship*, as shown in Figure 3.4.

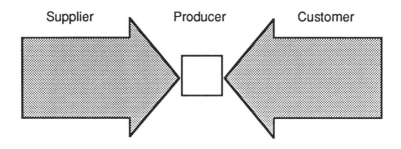

Figure 3.3
Dependent Relationship

In an independent relationship, you might not acknowledge any help from anyone for a brilliant idea that was all yours. You may be the Russian Republic who thought it could "go it alone." You may be a John Wayne, single-handedly taming the West! Independence ranges from individual brilliance to what Dr. Deming calls rugged individualism.

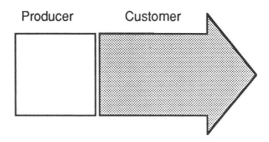

Figure 3.4
Independent Relationship

If you balance the independence of the producer with dependence on suppliers and on customers, that process relationship is an *interdependent relationship.* There are many such situations. I mentioned in Chapter 1 that our lives are filled with interdependent networks of customer and supplier transactions. We all need to be a part of a family or a team within society.

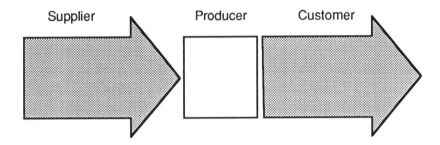

Figure 3.5
Interdependent Relationship

All of us must grow out of dependent relationships and into a balanced combination of independence and interdependence. The maturing process in western cultures proceeds from the dependent to the independent and has had a difficult time with interdependence in formal processes. The process of maturation in eastern cultures, on the other hand, grows from dependence to interdependence and, conversely, has a difficult time with independence.

The simple matrix in Figure 3.6 summarizes my theory for change. This matrix should not be interpreted to mean that the ideal state is in the lower right-hand corner. Rather there is a need to mature from Dependence to a *balance* of Independent and Interdependent process relationships in all three categories of change. I recently read Stephen Covey's book[16] and found that he also considers these categories to be important. But while he considers interdependence as the ideal, I see a very compelling need for balance between independence and interdependence.

	Dependent	Independent	Interdependent
Physical	Do It For Me	I Do It	We Do It
Logical	Teach Me	I Understand What I Do	I Understand How What I Do Helps Optimize Process
Emotional	Love Me	Joy In Work: I Feel Important	Joy In Belonging To A Team

Figure 3.6
A Matrix of Process Relationships

---

[16]Stephen R. Covey, *The 7 Habits of Highly Effective People* (New York: Simon & Schuster, 1989).

Remember that there is no hierarchy between the physical, logical, or emotional levels of the mind. Not only must all of the categories be incorporated within proposed changes, but independence and interdependence must be included as well. Finally, barriers to change, which are implicit within the categories themselves, must be overcome.

Physical barriers:

Dr. Deming writes about the golfer who cannot improve his game because he is already in the state of statistical control. He points out that you have only one chance to train a person. Someone whose skill level is in statistical control, will have great difficulty improving his skills. The only hope for such an individual lies within the Method for Continual Improvement. Sometimes significant physical events, such as Japan losing World War II; the threat of being hanged in the morning (as described by Samuel Johnson); or famous and crucial experiments, such as Foucault's pendulum[17] (which changed the body of science overnight), are in themselves sufficient to become agents of change on the physical level.

Logical barriers:

Change in the logical category has similar patterns, although statistical control has little to do with them. A person will tend to believe a theory or logical

---

[17]Thomas Kuhn, *The Essential Tension* (Chicago: University Press, 1977).

construct long after it has been disproven. In school, students accept theories, not because they necessarily understand them, but because they are presented with the authority of the teacher (physical), or because they trust the teacher (emotional). Again, William Ouchi writes about what he calls superstitious learning:

> It is like the knowledge of a primitive tribe that if they perform a ritual each night, they will cause the sun to return twelve hours hence. Superstitious learning is difficult to overcome. ... Over time, those rational beliefs that are most central to a community will take on an ethical and moral quality (emotional), which will serve to integrate those central beliefs into communal life more fully and which will protect them from change.[18]

Daniel Boorstin relates that:

> ... the great obstacle to discovering the shape of the earth, the continents, and the ocean was not ignorance, but the illusion of knowledge.[19]

We *know* a lot and are loathe to give up our mistaken knowledge. Daniel T. Gilbert writes:

> Much of the recent research converges on a single point: people are credulous creatures who find it very easy to believe and very difficult to doubt.[20]

Sometimes a significant logical event enables us

---

[18]William Ouchi, The M-Form Society (Reading: Addison-Wesley, 1984).

[19]Daniel Boorstin, *The Discoverers: A History of Man's Search to Know His World and Himself* (New York: Vintage Books Division of Random House, 1985).

[20]Bruce Bower, "True Believers," Science News, 5 Jan. 1991, © 1991 by Science Services, Inc. (Used with permission).

to change our theory: "Eureka! I finally understand!" Dr. Deming considers the Red Bead and Funnel Experiments to be significant logical events. He says to managers, "This should change the way you approach management. You may even have to ride home with people that do not know these things."

Emotional barriers:

Not surprisingly, the barriers to change in the emotional category are similar to the barriers in the physical and logical. A person will tend to remember his or her first love or first hate. The initial emotional bonds that are formed can take a long time to change and then re-form with others. Significant emotional events are more widely known than significant logical events or significant physical events. This is probably because the latter have not been defined before. The philosopher Ernst Cassirer once took his ten-year old daughter to her first opera. As they left "Figaro," the little girl was deeply surprised to find that her beloved Berlin was very different from when they entered the Opera House. Everything had changed. Another little girl, after hearing Beethoven's Ninth Symphony for the first time, asked "What must we do now?" Rilke, in his "Ode to Archaic Apollo," wrote of the effect of seeing the statue for the first time. He ends with, "You must change your life."[21]

Section Two will help you do just that.

---

[21]L. Leshan and H. Margenau, *Einstein's Space and Van Gogh's Sky* (New York: Collier Books, 1982).

SECTION TWO

OPERATIONALIZING THE DEMING PHILOSOPHY ... EVOLUTION IN PRACTICE

Operationalizing
The Deming Philosophy...
Evolution in Practice

Understanding the Deming Philosophy is a revolution in thought, even though many people call it plain common sense. It certainly is not common—yet —but it does make sense. Thomas Kuhn observed that in scientific revolutions, the rejection of one paradigm must be accompanied by the acceptance of another.

We have seen that history consistently shows change taking place on three levels: Physical, Logical, and Emotional. One might quickly reorganize the People and buy new Equipment and low cost Material (Physical), but it may take longer to put in place the Methods to get them to understand the *why* (Logical), and it will take an entirely different approach to create the Environment that facilitates the "buy-in" (Emotional) needed for change.

I have used these three categories of change while helping organizations operationalize the philosophy of Dr. Deming. I have used them in the improvement of processes that leaders manage. Dr. Deming has said for years that the big problems, or the processes most in need of improvement, don't walk in your door. You must be out there looking for them. People are already doing their best. They can only solve the problems that they see—and try to solve those as best they can.

The chapters in this section are structured to make obvious what must be done in order to expand on the positive things, thoughts, and feelings that must be accomplished, and to eliminate the negative things, thoughts, and feelings of people *just doing their best.*

Chapter 4

Physical Change

There are numerous methods that can be used to affect change on the Physical level. Organization, Policies, Procedures, Standards, Specifications, Law, Measurements, Skills and Training, Rewards and Punishments are all forms of Physical change. They are tangible, quick, and relatively easy. But they are not sufficient in themselves for the kind of change that is needed.

Organization is but one form of the physical level of change. It is a physical level of change because if you report to me, we will be a team: we will cooperate, or we will accomplish some task because I hired you, I do your evaluation, and I can fire you. Changes in organizational reporting relationships can be accomplished with ease. We can quickly change offices, locations for work, our bosses, our subordinates, our associates, our other suppliers, our other customers. Other aspects of change are not so quick. Changes in organization may be necessary, but in themselves, they are not sufficient to produce a lasting change.

I stated in Chapter 1 that we all live and work in an interdependent network of processes. There are untold numbers of what I call micro-transactions of customers and suppliers.

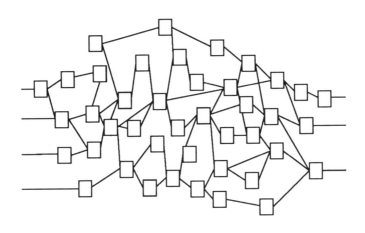

Figure 4.1
Interdependent Network of Processes

Early leaders found it difficult to achieve order out of the chaos of large groups of people without imposing a structure on them. Leaders, whether Moses, the Roman legions, the railroad barons, Max Weber, or Fredrick Taylor, have all tried to establish order by organizational structure. Post industrial revolution organizations also expected to develop functional expertise. As a result of their efforts, departments of accountants, engineers, assemblers, marketers, and the like were formed.

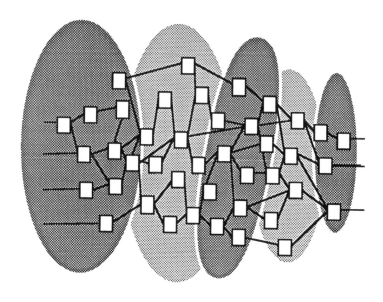

Figure 4.2
Network Organized by Function

This functionally oriented organization is called the U-Form by William Ouchi. It is a unified organization that can only operate as one entity. No subgrouping of it can stand alone.[1] The engineers could not operate by themselves, nor could the accountants or any of the other functional organizations. The strength of this organization is the cultivation of excellence within the various functional boundaries. But in order for the organization to operate, much less excel, there must be a way to conduct transactions between the functional boundaries. There must be communication between

[1]William Ouchi, *The M-Form Society*, (Reading: Addison-Wesley, 1984).

designers, engineers, manufacturers, marketers, and purchasers. If the U-Form organization does not facilitate these needed interactions, what should you do?

Reorganize!

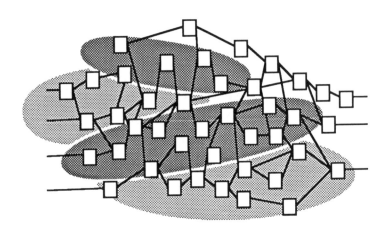

Figure 4.3
Network Organized by Project

Teams can be reorganized from single function departments to multi-functional projects. Often, the top functional people are already grouped together in multi-functional teams. Engineers, manufacturing people, buyers, quality control people, accountants, and even statisticians can all be on simultaneous engineering teams. The strength of this organization is the multi-functional focus on the excellence of a particular project.

But for this organization to prosper, there must be communication between, as well as within, the pro-

ject teams. The project boundaries and allegiances inhibit this communication. What should be done?

Reorganize!

But they just did that!

In statistical terms, both of these organizations
minimize (or optimize) the within-subgroup variability,
no matter how the subgroup is defined. The problem is
that they also suboptimize the between-subgroup variability. An effective and efficient organization needs to
optimize both. Merely rearranging the boundaries
often trades one suboptimization for another. Reorganization is easy and vitally necessary, but it is no
panacea for improvement.

A fabrication plant that was part of one division
did all of its business with an assembly plant from another division. They had problems with both quality
and delivery. Each plant felt that the other was not
cooperating. Since the problems were not resolved,
higher levels of management stepped in, looked around
and reorganized. The fabrication plant now reported
to the same division that the assembly plant did.
Management thought that if they reported to the same
person—that if they were in the same organization—
the problems of lack of cooperation would go away.
They did not. They have not. And I think they will
not. As always, there are more than just physical organizational issues involved in this situation.

A similar example involves engineers from an
outside design firm. The customer company could not
manage to make their work a priority for the outside
engineers. Since the engineers worked for someone

else, the customer company was also concerned about their possible lack of allegiance. The solution seemed obvious: hire the engineers away from the supplier. Supposedly, when the engineers "physically belonged" to the customer company, the problems would go away. They did not. They have not. And I think they will not. The red beads that affected the priorities had nothing to do with physical reporting relationships, but with conflicting and changing priorities within the customer company.

Start-up organizations, or high growth organizations, must be able to reorganize their processes in order to grow. There are also times to regroup and contract in any organization. It is not simply a Physical level decision to determine what the optimum size of an organization should be. Although most of these reorganization changes are obviously on the Physical level, sometimes they operate on the Mental or Logical level. Peter Drucker observes that a crucial mistake often made by a start-up company occurs when the founder does not learn to become the "leader of a team." Instead, he continues to operate on the more physically-oriented "star with helpers" mentality.[2]

There is a lot of talk that the secret of Japanese management is found in their "strong" managers. "Strong" is interpreted to mean people in possession of complete authority and responsibility, with all of the necessary resources reporting to them. I think it is a mistake to try to organize according to such a simple conclusion. Managers never have all resources totally

---

[2]Peter F. Drucker, *Innovation and Entrepreneurship*, (London: HarperCollins, 1986).

under their control. A "strong" program manager is one who is able to command (Physical), convince (Logical), and inspire (Emotional) those over whom he has no direct Physical control.

One company initiated a major project to improve the engineering, manufacturing, and purchasing processes. The Vice President for Purchasing was "strong," and so was designated as project manager. But he had no chance to deliver an improved process unless he could convince his peers, the Vice President for Engineering and the Vice President for Manufacturing (people over whom he had no direct control) that they had an equity in participating in the process.

The temptation to reorganize when things are bad, and avoid reorganization when things seem good, is often overpowering. Reorganization does not just involve People: you can also reorganize Equipment or Material flow. Work place organization and visual controls are simple physical techniques for change. They are the same things. Do not expect Physical level changes to be a "silver bullet" or "instant pudding," (as Dr. Deming calls it). Simultaneous engineering strategies are not ends in themselves; the organization would not necessarily work better if every employee worked in the same room. These reorganizations are beneficial if they introduce you to internal customers and suppliers whom you did not know existed. But there is no substitute for unraveling the dynamics of the interdependent network of customers and suppliers through a continuing series of process flow diagrams.

Organization for Guidance on Quality

Dr. Deming has, for years, urged the establishment of the position of "Leader of Statistical Methodology" in every organization. Right now he prefers the
title, "Leader of Profound Knowledge" or simply, "Aide
to the Chairman."

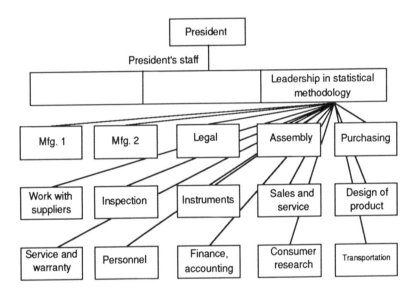

Figure 4.4
Organization Chart Including
A Leader of Statistical Methodology

The Leader of Profound Knowledge must be on the job. And it is not a part-time job! All of Dr. Deming's examples got into the books *because he was there to help.* The people did not recognize the need for improvement. They were only "doing their best." Mencius said:

> Don't suspect that the king lacks wisdom. Even in the case of things that grow most easily in the world, they would never grow up if they were exposed to sunshine for one day and then to cold for ten days. It is seldom that I have an audience with him, and when I leave, others who expose him to cold arrive. Even if what I say to him is taking root, what good does it do?[3]

This innovation took a long time to gain acceptance. It was easy to assign statisticians to plants, or even to a Division. But there was some reluctance to create a position which reported to the top leader of the organization. Statisticians were not considered to be in the mainstream of disciplines which needed to be represented at the highest levels. This is changing: the US Census Bureau, Ford, General Motors, Nashua Corporation, Albany International, Navistar, and others do have statisticians reporting to the highest levels in their organization.

What do they do? How can they help? I will give you my perspective as one who holds the position.

---

[3]Wing-Tsit Chan, *A Sourcebook in Chinese Philosophy*, (Princeton: Princeton University Press, 1963).

First of all, we are leaders; leaders of statistical methodology, or leaders of profound knowledge, or aides to the Chairman. The aim of our leadership should be to improve the performance of man and machine, to improve quality, to increase output, and to simultaneously bring pride of workmanship to people.[4] We must also have the same characteristics that any leader should possess. I have taken some attributes of a leader, as defined by Dr. Deming, combined them with his views on profound knowledge (the subject of Chapter 5), and added my own perspectives to come up with some specifics pertaining to the attributes required for the position.

Attributes of a Leader of Profound Knowledge

Creates more leaders:

Dr. Deming has not rank-ordered these attributes, but I think it is important first to stress the continuation of the species, or in other words, to insure the immortality of the leader. At present, there is a severe shortage of "leaders of profound knowledge." There is no shortage of statisticians—or psychologists —or facilitators. But when all qualities must be combined within one person, a dramatic shortage is evident. Very few universities have made the major changes to their curriculum that would develop stu-

---

[4] W. Edwards Deming, *Out of the Crisis* (Cambridge: MIT CAES, 1986), page 248.

dents of "Profound Knowledge." The few that I know about include: Columbia University, Fordham University, Oakland University, The University of Miami, The University of Michigan, and The University of Tennessee.

Because the educational system does not produce "Leaders of Profound Knowledge," industry must engage in the costly retraining (rework) of people. I will discuss the various educational training courses and processes available in industry and academia in Chapter 5.

Within Ford and General Motors, I have formed organizations whose purpose is to develop the statistical profession within the company. Later in this chapter, I will discuss the Statistical Methods Office, the Statistical Methods Council, the "Gang," and the "Crowd." You need to build a professional career ladder for your people because, more than likely, none exists for statisticians in your organization.

Focuses on the customer:

Your primary customers are the other formal and informal leaders in your organization. A formal leader is one who occupies an official position of leadership. An informal leader leads through knowledge or personality. Other customers include Quality and Organizational Development disciplines. It is very easy to spend your valuable time solving problems that people bring to you. You must do market research to find the leaders with whom you need to spend your time. You must do a bit of triage here. Some will ask for your help, others you will have to ask, and still others you must leave alone, for they are only a waste of your time. I prefer to focus—not to use a shotgun.

Knows when to coach and when to judge:

I have modified Dr. Deming's statement of, "Coach and counsel. Do not be a judge and a jury." I think this is a matter of balance. To coach and counsel is an off-line process and part of the Voice of the Process. To Judge is an on-line process and part of the Voice of the Customer. If you have only one shot, or you are "in extremis," you might get away with being a judge and a jury. In fact, if it becomes necessary, you have a professional obligation to speak up and perhaps even to stop the line. For the most part, however, you need to coach and counsel, encouraging your customers to improve. Because it is off-line, this approach is less threatening.

To be an effective coach and counselor, you must establish a professional-to-client relationship with customers. It is vital for them to know that you are not, without their permission, discussing your counseling sessions with others. When dealing with a client's supervisor, the balance becomes even more delicate. You must not betray confidences of your clients. For instance, a vice president who understood what needs to be done and asked the right questions when Dr. Deming or I were around, sometimes acted far differently after we left. You must counsel in a manner that is specific enough for this kind of individual and yet not betray confidences.

Removes obstacles to joy in work:

There are major processes that stand in the way of joy of ownership or workmanship. Quality management, financial considerations, appraisal of employees, compensation, and general management are just a few. The removal of obstacles is not enough. Every process must be improved so that it encourages people to take joy in their work—which will enable customers to take joy in their ownership. Since many of them directly affect the emotional level, I will discuss these processes in detail in Chapter 6.

Understands variation:

From the customer's perspective, all variation is the same: it is bad. From the process manager's perspective, variation is composed of special and common causes. You must understand both perspectives, the Voice of the Customer and the Voice of the Process. The red bead experiment can help you explain the difference. I will further discuss variation in Chapter 5.

Works to improve the system:

Because you have profound knowledge, you use the Deming Cycle (PDSA), not serendipity or "experience" to improve your customers' processes. Some trips through the Cycle result in setbacks; other trips result in no apparent change; others result in improvement. The funnel experiment can help you make this point. Again, I will discuss more of the details of PDSA in Chapter 5. A statistician must be a historian so that leaders may work on the future. Professor William Ouchi urges the use of social memory to optimize the process. One trip through the improvement cycle is a "snapshot"; continual improvement requires that you string the snapshots together.

Creates trust:

I like the definition of trust used by William Ouchi. It is very simple and does not depend on someone else. It starts with you. It is your willingness to owe someone else a favor. You trust that he will not call in the favor at a time inopportune to you. Accepting help is not a sign of weakness. Get help from other leaders and professionals. When you are owed the favor, you can also build trust by not calling it due at an inopportune time for your debtor.

Forgives a mistake:

There will be false starts, obstacles, and problems with everyone just "doing his best." When a person makes a mistake, make sure you understand the individual's contribution to the problem, in relation to the rest of the process, including all interactions between People, Materials, Methods, Equipment, and Environment. For a person who feels blameless, the only thing worse than assigning blame is to give forgiveness!

Listens:

Two thousand years ago, Epictetus said, "God gave man two ears, but only one mouth, that he might hear twice as much as he speaks."[5] You cannot give useful advice unless you listen to what your customers are saying. You should not be giving the answers; you should be asking the questions and then questioning the answers. There will be plenty of time to demonstrate your knowledge. Peter Scholtes talks about the benefits of active listening.[6] He suggests that you rephrase what you thought you heard. This encourages the customer to talk even more so that you might better understand him. G. K. Chesterton wrote:

> There are some people—and I am one of them— who think that the most practical and important thing about a man is still his view of the universe. We think that for a landlady considering a lodger it is important to know his income, but still more important to know his philosophy. We think that for a general about to fight an enemy it is important to know the enemy's numbers, but still more important to know the enemy's philosophy.[7]

---

[5]Diane Ackerman, *A Natural History of the Senses*, (New York: Vintage Books, 1990).
[6]Peter Scholtes, *The Team Handbook* (Madison: Joiner Associates, 1988).
[7]William James, *Pragmatism* (New York: Harvard University Press, 1947).

I think that it is also important for a leader to listen—
in order to discern a person's philosophy.

Continually improves his education:

I have mentioned previously that the biggest
barrier to the improvement of knowledge is the illusion
of knowledge. I have personally found it very difficult
to continue my formal education because of my position
of leadership. People expect me to know all the questions—as well as the answers. I continue to learn by
reading and informal study and conversations with the
great people I meet. One of the more profound learnings that I have garnered from Dr. Deming is that you
are never too old, or too important, or too learned to
stop learning. I also think it applies to teaching as
well. One of Dr. Deming's favorite questions to leaders
is "What have you done to improve your education?"
Without exception, their answers focus on what they
have done to approve money and time for the education of their people. This is commendable, but should
not be a priority until the leader advances his own education. It is sad how often we confuse delegation with
"getting it out of my office."

It is obvious that every organization is different.
Each has its strengths and weaknesses. The strength
of General Motors is in its people. It is also our weakness. I have never seen a company with so many
skilled, intelligent, and talented individuals. But our
greatest challenge is to foster a sense of **Teamwork**.
We do have small teams, but they are suboptimized. I

think that because we grew by acquisition, our allegiances may still be with New Departure, Packard, Chevrolet, Buick, Delco, Remy, EDS, Oldsmobile, Opel, AC Spark Plug, Inland, Oakland, Pontiac, Hughes, Vauxhall, Fisher Body, Cadillac, Allison, GMAC, Electro-Motive, Truck and Coach, Holden's, Hyatt Roller Bearing, Hydra-Matic, Rochester, Saab, and Central Staffs.

This is nothing new. Alfred P. Sloan, Jr. wrote:

> ... one of the obstacles to integrating the various divisions was the fact that key executives had little incentive to think in terms of the welfare of the whole corporation. On the contrary, the general managers were encouraged to think primarily of their own division's profits ... The Bonus Plan established the concept of corporate profit in place of divisional profits, which only incidentally added up to the corporation's net income.[8]

I agree with Sloan's thinking: he needed to emphasize the corporate team. He instituted a policy that Physically rewarded team players. Unfortunately, the operational definition of any policy is not what the writer intends, but what actually happens when the policy is carried out. This policy did affect change in some, but not in those who needed Logical and Emotional reinforcement.

---

[8]Alfred P. Sloan, Jr., *My Years With General Motors*, (Garden City: Anchor Press, 1972).

You might say that General Motors did just fine with the policy. They expanded and improved. But as Dr. Deming has said for years, "Don't confuse success with success." Ask yourself how much better the plan could have been if there had been optimization on all three levels.

That (optimization on all three levels) is now the plan for GM. Our overall model for running the business takes the physical form of a triangle, appropriately balancing the Physical, Logical, and Emotional.

Figure 4.5
Business Model of General Motors

The Vision of General Motors:

To be the 21st century company building and marketing the world's greatest cars and trucks.

The Mission of General Motors

To provide products and services of such quality that our customers will receive superior value, our employes[9] and business partners will share in our success, and our stockholders will receive a sustained, superior return on their investment.

I have learned that the physical statement that communicates your constancy of purpose should be value-oriented. Values are able to withstand the test of time. Furthermore, they are already internalized in every human being and only need to be externalized, or operationalized, in a consistent manner.

General Motors Beliefs and Values

Customer Satisfaction through People - We believe that the people of GM are its greatest strength. Through their dedication and commitment to excellence, our people are the key to achieving our customer satisfaction goals.

Customer Satisfaction through Teamwork - Joined as a team in a spirit of cooperation, union, management, hourly, and salaried employes are working to achieve a common goal - customer satisfaction.

---

[9]This is not misspelled. This is the way GM spells "employee."

Customer Satisfaction through Continuous Improvement - The people of GM are committed to the concept of continuous improvement in everything we do.

Objectives, Strategies, Initiatives, Goals

The specifics of these are proprietary. They flow from the Vision, Mission, and Values of the company. Quite predictably they balance four major characteristics of any organization: Quality, Cost, Timeliness, and Greatness. They also balance the Physical, Logical, and Emotional levels. They progress from Dependent to Independent and Interdependent. They balance the short-term with the long-term. And they are even beginning to balance North America with the rest of the world.

For the first time in General Motor's history, the Quality organization reports to the Chairman. The intent of this change is obvious. Quality applies to everything we do and everywhere we do it. Whether it is electronics, diesel locomotives, financial services, cars, or trucks: all are affected by quality. In Eastern or Western Europe, Australia, Asia, Africa, South America or North America: all are affected by quality.

The UAW/General Motors' Quality Network has provided the structure to improve quality through its quality councils at the corporate, group, division, and local levels. Training, in a variety of socio-technical tools and skills, will be accomplished by an interdependent network of training organizations, all having a consistent strategic focus, but able to operationalize that direction locally. The core subject matter comes from over 30 Action Strategies that teams of GM/UAW people have developed over the past two years.

One of the Action Strategies is Statistical Methodology. On the Physical Level, it calls for the establishment of a Statistical Methodology Organization reporting to the highest levels in the Company. To prepare for this, a team of people have developed a Mission Statement for the organization.

Mission: Statistical and Process Improvement Methods Organization

Within the framework of the Quality Network, provide direction for the consistent practice of continual improvement of processes so that all GM employes, suppliers and dealers can take joy in delivering the highest quality customer-valued products and services. We will accomplish this by:

- Delivering appropriate education and training,

- Consulting to improve all processes and to demonstrate the use of the methods, and

- Coaching key individuals to lead the improvement of processes which inhibit others from improving.

A Mission Statement should recognize that people learn in different ways. I remember Phil Caldwell, the former Chairman of Ford Motor Company, commenting that every word weighs a ton. Each word was chosen for a specific reason. So in addition to the Mission Statement, we included some background information that begins to explain our choice of words. It is an attempt on the physical level to link with the logical and emotional levels. We must not only follow the letter of the law, but the spirit of it as well.

**Further Explanation of
Key Words and Phrases in the Mission**

Quality Network:

The one GM process of institutionalizing our People, Beliefs and Values to achieve total customer satisfaction through people, teamwork and continual improvement.

Direction:

Implies proactive participation with our customers. **Guidance, recommendation,** or **suggestion** are all too passive. We intend to be partners with our customers and not wash our hands of them if they don't take our advice.

Consistent Practice:

Over time, the smallest possible variation in the exercise of an occupation or profession. **Application** or **use** do not imply the profound knowledge needed to actually improve processes and reduce cost.

Continual Improvement:

Getting better and better by bringing the Voice of the Customer and the Voice of the Process closer and closer.

Processes:

The value-added blending of People, Materials, Methods, Machines, and Environment to produce a product or service for a customer. Systems are synonymous with processes. Every person manages processes no matter where they are or what they do. They are all customers and they are all suppliers in an interdependent network of processes. There are two sources of communication in a process: the Voice of the Customer and the Voice of the Process.

Employes, suppliers, and dealers:

Literally everyone associated with our products and services.

Joy:

In order for our customers to have joy of ownership, we must be able to take joy in our work. This implies that each of us identifies, understands, and empathizes what it is going to take to get our customers to delight in owning our products and services. We must also change processes that inhibit joy of workmanship to processes that foster joy of workmanship.

Customer-valued:

The customer determines value. It is of little use for us to meet our internal specifications or requirements if the customer does not take joy in owning our products and services. We predict what the customer wants and desires through the Voice of the Customer.

Products and Services:

The outcomes of a process. Many people in service/administrative/management processes have difficulty recognizing that they deliver a product to a customer. So we use both words to denote the outcomes of a process. Those outcomes are also inputs to subsequent processes.

Delivering appropriate education and training:

Delivery implies:

- defining customer needs and expectations,
- determining the process to educate and train, and
- developing suitably-qualified teachers.

Education is knowledge-based while training is skills-based. Education and training include a variety of socio-technical process improvement tools and are not limited to "statistical methods."

Consulting to improve all processes and to demonstrate the use of the methods:

Knowledge and skills are vital, but only if people use them. To effectively use them, we must go beyond education and training for two reasons:

- In order to effectively teach, we must be practicing professionals.
- In order to take the first step, people need "active encouragement" to use their newly acquired knowledge or skill.

Coaching key individuals to lead the improvement of processes which inhibit others from improving:

An earlier version of this focused on the removal of inhibitors. We now know that a lack of a negative does not indicate a strong positive. We must have processes that encourage improvement. It is very important to identify key people in the organization who have leverage for change. They are the informal as well as the formal leaders and must understand, use and champion the new philosophy. Many times they manage systems that inhibit others from improving or otherwise from taking pride in their work. These systems include:

- People development and compensation systems
- Financial management systems
- Product development systems, and
- Quality management systems, just to name a few.

The big opportunities do not walk in our door. We must be an integral part of major decision processes so that we can identify opportunities for improvement that others cannot be expected to see. It is our responsibility then to coach the leaders so that they might learn from our perspective. We are not presumptuous to think that ours is the only perspective, just that it is a necessary one for improvement.

At the beginning of 1991, there were over 200 salaried and UAW employees of General Motors who were qualified, active members of the Statistical Methodology network. The "Gang" consists of about 15 statisticians from all over the Company who are appointed by their respective Group Vice Presidents. We meet monthly to coordinate the operationalization of our Mission Statement. The "Crowd" consists of the rest of the 200 who are assigned to the various divisions, plants and offices. We meet quarterly for coordination, planning, and development purposes.

Another very necessary and enabling document for many at General Motors is the 1990 GM-UAW Contract Settlement Agreement document, or "The Book." Prior to the 1990 contract, Quality was considered by both sides to be so basic that it was above the negotiation process. Therefore, it was not included in The Book. I think both sides realized that a number of people, from both labor and management, were not participating in necessary improvement activities for the simple reason that *it was not in The Book*. It is there now, and this will enable the participation of those who were previously hesitant to join. This is necessary for some, but not sufficient for others.

The specific approach I have taken at General Motors is different from the one I took at Ford. The model for change is the same, but different organizations require different kinds of applications.

The strength of Ford Motor Company is their sense of team or family. It is also their weakness. The company needs to attract and *retain* more of "the best and brightest." There are many companies who are very appreciative to Ford for its alumni.

It took Ford about two years to develop its constancy of purpose statement: its Mission, Values and Guiding Principles. We started in 1983 and it was introduced to the Company in November, 1984 in Boca Raton, by Henry Ford II in his farewell speech to the leadership of the company.

Ford Motor Company
Mission, Values, and Guiding Principles

Mission:

Ford Motor Company is a worldwide leader in automotive and automotive-related products and services as well as in newer industries such as aerospace, communications, and financial services. Our mission is to improve continually our products and services to meet our customers' needs, allowing us to prosper as a business and to provide a reasonable return for our stockholders, the owners of our business.

Values:

How we accomplish our mission is as important as the mission itself. Fundamental to success for the Company are these basic values:

- **People** - Our people are the source of our strength. They provide our corporate intelligence and determine our reputation and vitality. Involvement and teamwork are our core human values.

- **Products** - Our products are the end result of our efforts, and they should be the best in serving customers worldwide. As our products are viewed, so are we viewed.

- **Profits** - Profits are the ultimate measure of how efficiently we provide customers with the best products for their needs. Profits are required to survive and grow.

Guiding Principles :

- **Quality comes first** - To achieve customer satisfaction, the quality of our products and services must be our number one priority.

- **Customers are the focus of everything we do** - Our work must be done with customers in mind, providing better products and services than our competition.

- **Continuous improvement is essential to our success** - We must strive for excellence in everything we do: in our products, in their safety and value - and in our services, our human relations, our competitiveness, and our profitability.

- **Employee involvement is our way of life** - We are a team. We must treat each other with trust and respect.

- **Dealers and suppliers are our partners** - The Company must maintain mutually beneficial relationships with dealers, suppliers, and our other business associates.

- **Integrity is never compromised** - The conduct of our Company worldwide must be pursued in a manner that is socially responsible and commands respect for its integrity and for its positive contributions to society. Our doors are open to men and women alike without discrimination and without regard to ethnic origin or personal beliefs.

You can easily see the influence of Dr. Deming in the Guiding Principles statement. They originally started out as the 14 Points but we found that a Constancy of Purpose Statement should have some familiarity to the organization: it must build on the good that has gone before. So we used terminology already known by Ford people: Quality is Job 1, Employee Involvement, Integrity. To these we added, Dr. Deming's concepts of Continual Improvement, suppliers and dealers as partners, and the pleasing of customers.

Ford uses a lot of 3x5 cards to convey information and important information is laminated. The Mission, Values, and Guiding Principles were on a laminated 3x5 card, and you didn't leave home without it. This little piece of physical level change provided many employees the licence to take the card out at meetings or discussions if they were getting too far off course. Bob Stempel, Chairman of General Motors, periodically pulls our Beliefs and Values Statement from his coat pocket and everybody in the room gets the message. Even simple messages take time to deploy in large organizations. Donald Petersen, former Chairman of Ford, commiserated that:

> There is a communications factor that cannot be
> overestimated, and that is I find I must repeat
> myself time and time and time again because of
> the very size of the enterprise of which you are
> dealing.[10]

James K. Bakken, Vice President of Operations Staffs for Ford, and now retired, was the driving force for implementing Dr. Deming's recommendation that Ford needed to establish an Office of Statistical Methodology. If he had not found a way to fund the effort, I believe it would have been impossible to accomplish what we did. We needed people and resources to operationalize our Charter.

Charter of the Statistical Methods Office
Ford Motor Company

The Charter of the Statistical Methods Office is to facilitate the application of statistical thinking in support of the Company's Mission, Values, and Guiding Principles within the Company, its supply base, and its dealer organizations.

The responsibilities of the Office are to:

* Develop, maintain, and improve statisticians (Associates, Statistical Methods Council Members, and external resources) who act as partners and catalysts for the Company's improvement.

---

[10]"The Deming Library,"Vol. III, (Chicago: Films Inc., 1987).

- Provide consultation in the application of statistical and improvement methods.

- Develop and maintain for the Company a basic approach to education and training and institutionalization of statistical methods.

The Associates remain members of the Statistical Methods Office to maximize consistency of approach, facilitate the exchange of experience, and otherwise enhance communication and dissemination of best methods. The Statistical Methods Office also provides broad direction and administrative and other support in the institutionalization of Ford Total Quality Excellence.

The Statistical Methods Council at Ford (Figure 4.6) consisted of statisticians from the various divisions in the company. These statisticians were appointed by the General Managers of their various divisions. The purpose of the Council was to act as a resource for the Total Quality Excellence Committee, composed of key General Managers and Vice Presidents from all of Ford. The Statistical Methods Council also met monthly to plan and review improvement efforts.

If I could start from the beginning, I would organize for Quality along Physical, Logical, and Emotional lines. Reporting to the Vice President for Quality would be a Leader of Quality Promotion, a Leader of Profound Knowledge, and a Leader of Quality Process, as shown in Figure 4.7.

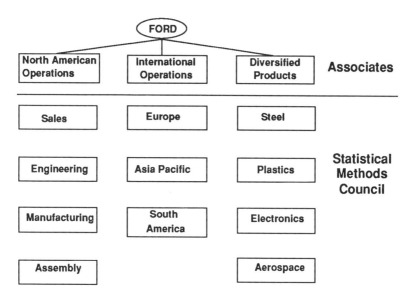

Figure 4.6
The Statistical Methods Council
of Ford Motor Company

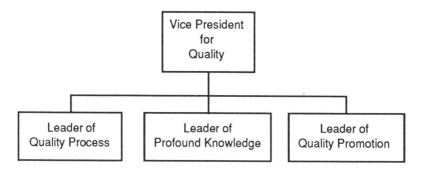

Organization for Quality
Figure 4.7

The Vice President for Quality is the Chairman's chief advisor for quality. The Leader of Quality Process coordinates measurements, audits, reports, and standards. These activities should be balanced throughout the product development cycle, and not be concentrated in production. The Leader of Profound Knowledge coordinates the education and training for quality, stays at the cutting edge of quality methodology, advances questions that increase knowledge, and fulfills the attributes that I described earlier in this chapter. The Leader of Quality Promotion coordinates the communication of the quality message to both external and internal customers.

Skills and Training

Skills and Training are a key to physical level change. They are closely linked to Education and knowledge which I will discuss in Chapter 5. We all need to develop skills in order to operationalize the Method for Continual Improvement. You need skills in each step. No one skill is useful for all steps, but many good ones are shown in Figure 4.8.

I have developed simple pro formas for each of the steps (shown in Figures 4.9, 4.10, and 4.11). Together, they are similar to the QC storyboards that some organizations use. Process Management Institute has a particularly good approach . They not only provide for good internal consistency, but when filled out, they are useful physical and logical examples of improvement.

Dr. Myron Tribus has published a video taped series of lectures entitled "Deployment Flow Charting." I highly recommend it.

Tools	Steps in PDSA Cycle							
	1	2	3	4	5	6	7	8
Box and Whisker Plots						●		
Brainstorming			●	●			●	
Cause and Effect Diagrams		●		●			●	
Check Sheets				●				
Control Charts	●						●	
Creative Problem Solving				●			●	
Design of Experiments					●			
Failure Mode Analysis			●					
Failure Mode and Effects Analysis			●					
Fault Tree Analysis			●					
Force Field Analysis			●					
Gantt / Pie Charts				●				
Histograms and Run Charts	●					●		
Impact Matrices				●			●	
Listening	●	●		●		●	●	●
Loss Function	●					●		●
Operational Definitions	●			●		●		●
Pareto Diagrams				●				●
Process Flow Charts		●	●				●	
Quality Function Deployment	●			●		●		●
Regression Analysis	●			●	●	●		
Reliability Analysis					●			
Scatter Diagrams	●			●		●		
Simulation					●			
Surveys	●	●				●	●	
Systems Analysis				●	●			
Teambuilding				●			●	
Time Series Forecasting	●					●		
Visioning			●				●	

Figure 4.8
Techniques for the 8 Steps of the Deming Cycle

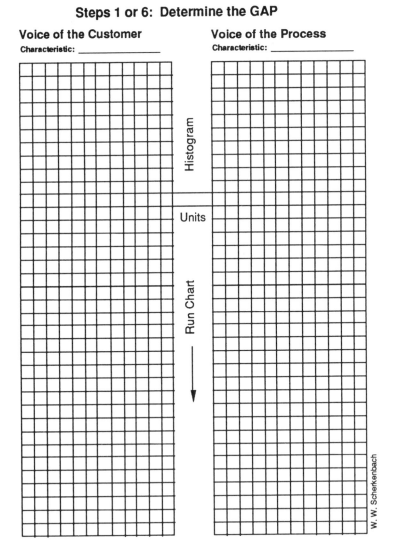

Figure 4.9
Form for Visualizing the GAP

Steps 2 or 3: Develop the MAPs

Map of the existing process or Map of the improved process

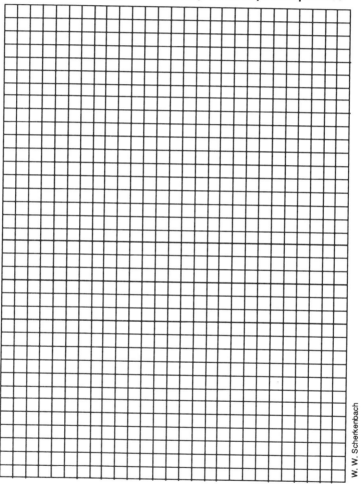

W. W. Scherkenbach

Figure 4.10
Form for Visualizing the MAP

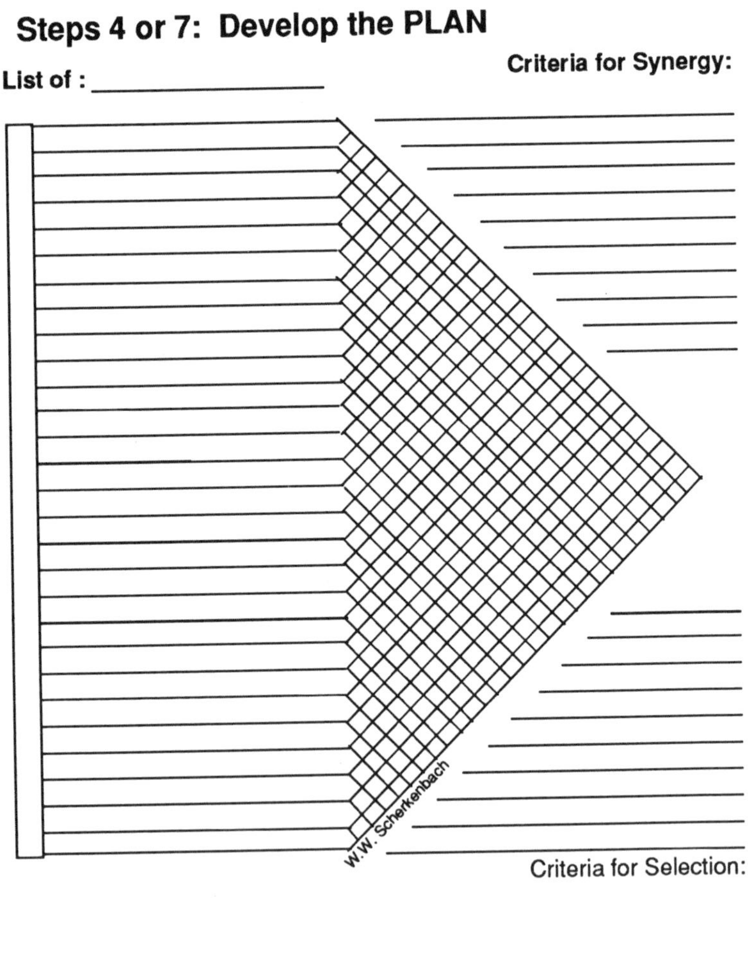

Steps 4 or 7: Develop the PLAN

List of : _____   Criteria for Synergy:

W.W. Scherkenbach

Criteria for Selection:

Figure 4.11
Form for Interlocking Action Matrix Measurements

Measurements

There are numerous measurable and not-so-measurable characteristics. While the measurements themselves are physical, what they measure may be physical, logical, or emotional. They are also characteristics that you might want to develop or inhibit. They include:

People: Joy, pride, delight, fear, anxiety, wellness, absence, grievance, doubt, competence, teamwork, knowledge, years of formal education, skills, years of apprenticeship, hours worked, number of people, years of seniority, age, weight, height, sex, race, income, religion, trust, integrity, despair, innovation, fidelity, industry, patience, wisdom, honesty, happiness, willingness to learn, responsibility, imagination, initiative, proactive, creative, introspection.

Method: (Some are better than others.) First In First Out(FIFO), Last In First Out(LIFO), First In Still Here(FISH), Ready Aim Fire, Plan-Do-Study-Act, Maintenance On Demand, Do Unto Others..., Don't Just Stand There Do Something, Don't Just Do Something Stand There, Prevention, Detection, Continual Improvement, ROA, ROE, ROI.

Material: Mass, weight, dimension, surface, color, odor, cost, sound, quality, durability, timeliness, taste, count, texture, velocity, acceleration.

Equipment: Mass, weight, dimension, color, odor, sound, uptime (MTTF), down-time (MTTR), cost, maintainability, durability, quality, timeliness, count.

Environment: Temperature, humidity, psychographics, demographics, morale, trust, fear, empowerment.

I cannot present these categories without a warning. They are a blend of the independent and interdependent. The independence is explicit in this portrayal; the interdependence is not. For this perspective, you must look from a different direction. A flow diagram is a better vehicle to show both independence and interdependence.

General Motors is in the process of evaluating the measurements that are required to run the company. This evaluation has so far uncovered over 2500 measurements that are sent to, and analyzed by, the corporate staff. The sheer number has required the provision of people to collect them, analyze them, report them, and file them.

In order to reduce the number of measurements, we have focused on our Corporate Beliefs and Values and the process model. We have recommended that about 60 highly interrelated measures be used instead of the 2500. GM is piloting these recommendations in 1991 and 1992. No measure may be used in isolation. Each affects, or is affected by, other measures.

The use of measurements as a set will help you better optimize efforts to please customers, whether they buy your vehicles, stock, or offer of employment.

Human Factors' Engineers have categorized the response of a customer into three groups: Physical, Cognitive, and Emotional. They further categorize the physical level into Control, Sensory-motor, and Anthropometric. It is very important to measure customers' responses on these levels in order to better target your design for product or service.

When we discuss operational definitions in Chapter 5, you will see that sensory input is vital for the development of theory that is useful in this world. I will discuss here some of the traditional 5 senses: taste, smell, sight, hearing, and touch. Each of these physical senses is intertwined with physical, logical and emotional responses as well.

Most words are rational in the sense that they must be understood to affect any response. If the word is spoken and not written, you have the opportunity to understand the word itself and the way it was spoken. If you do not understand the word or the symbol, if it is foreign to you, it is just noise. If you do understand, it can evoke responses on the physical, logical, and emotional levels.

Tones or notes, which are similar to letters, can also evoke responses on all three levels. But while each word in a verbal phrase tells something all by itself; musical tones or chords mean something only in relation to one another, when they're teamed up.[11] If the tones are considered music, they follow some pattern that is rational or pleasing to the listener, other-

---

[11]Diane Ackerman, *A Natural History of the Senses* (New York: Vintage Books, 1990).

wise they are perceived as noise. Music can trigger strong emotional responses as well as physical responses, the urge to dance or tap your foot comes to mind. Music can be used to help the inspection of large amounts of data. Notes from a recognizable musical score are paired with data. If a piece of data is out of control, a discordant note is played instead of the expected one. This combination of sight and sound performs better than sight or sound individually.

Smells are useful in education and training because they can enhance memory when associated with other sensory stimuli. Touch can be combined with sight to increase discrimination of inspection. All of the senses should be used in cases where measurement is otherwise too complex, or borders on the unknown and unknowable. People are truly your most important resource.

Rewards and Penalties

I prefer to use the concept of investment rather than reward or punishment. You can reward your pet for the completion of a trick. But I consider that to be demeaning to people. As you will see in Chapter 6, true motivation is intrinsic, not extrinsic. I speak of motivation because I assume that the reason for the reward or punishment is to reinforce some behavior or increase or decrease some characteristic of people mentioned on page 141. Your investment process must be flexible enough to optimize all business parameters.

Many times people who are not in top leadership positions recommend that those at the top be compensated according to Quality, not Quantity (or whatever it is that is looked on as good to do). I think that this might affect those who do the recommending, but it will not necessarily affect those at the top. We respond to physical, logical, and emotional cues differently at various points in time in our life. At one point in time we may feel important with more money, vacation, retirement points, a promotion, a vehicle, whatever. At other times we need more responsibility, power, recognition by peers. At still other times we are concerned with our immortality, our legacy, or our stewardship, our relationship with others. As I have said many times before, there is no hierarchy here. These cues can all be equally compelling. Some of the top leaders whom I have known in government, industry, labor, and academia would change their behavior for a bigger bonus, but many others most certainly would not. You should not move the funnel (Voice of the Process) without knowing where the target is (Voice of the Customer).

Policies, Procedures, Standards, and Specifications

These physical level products are helpful to some and a barrier to others. There are both positive and negative policies, procedures, standards, and specifications. I will discuss both. Trade barriers are one of the most obvious on the negative side.

Agricultural exports were once star performers for the United States in the balance of trade. Right now we import more than we export.

Dr. Deming once jokingly said to a Nobel Laureate economist that he thought it would be good for the government to buy up all the excess automobiles, as they do the excess agricultural products. It is a sad commentary that the economist thought it was a good idea. I am reminded of a concern of Adam Smith when he was attending the University of Oxford,

> where the greater part of the public professors have, for these many years, given up altogether even the pretence of teaching.

They taught Adam Smith one lesson he never forgot, the fate of any institution that did not depend on the goodwill of its customers.[12]

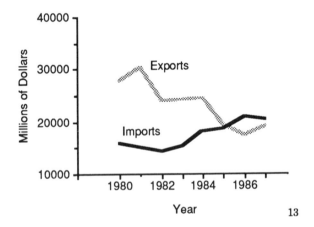

Figure 4.12
Agricultural Imports and Exports

---

[12]Daniel Boorstin, *The Discoverers: A History of Man's Search to Know His World and Himself* (New York: Vintage Books Division of Random House, 1985).
[13]Statistical Abstract of the U.S., 1989.

If there is a sector that has profited the most from statistical thinking, it is the agricultural sector. Started in the United Kingdom, Sir Ronald Fisher pioneered statistical experimentation at Rothhamsted. As a result of this, productivity in agriculture has been steadily increasing for decades. And yet why are so many farmers going out of business? *Because they have grown away from dependence on the goodwill of their customers.* They have become entangled with governments as not only their customers but also their suppliers.

Productivity improvements without quality improvements will only shift the cost of the apparent savings elsewhere. This suboptimization is furthered by the practices of grain exporting companies that encourage shipments of grain containing high dockage. A GAO study found that these companies consider themselves more efficient than those that ship higher quality grain because of lower dockage.[14] This is obviously short-sighted. The complaints from foreign customers are growing and the reputation of the United States in international markets is falling.

Even when the defects are eliminated, there must still be present the positives; the delighters; the matching of the Voice of the Process to the Voice of the Customer. You must deliver what the customer really wants. Dr. Deming said to the Japanese in 1950:

---

[14]"The Des Moines Register," George Anthan, June 11, 1986.

... it is a mistake to suppose that efficient production of product and service can, with certainty,
keep an organization solvent and ahead of its
competition. It is possible and, in fact, fairly easy
for an organization to go downhill and out of business making the wrong product or offering the
wrong type of service, even though everyone in the
organization performs with devotion, employing
statistical methods and every other aid that can
boost efficiency.[15]

Agriculture needs to anticipate and match the
changing needs of their customers. There have always
been regional preferences but you should see more
niches on the international level. Foods like designer
vegetables, or foods that enhance your health, or
nourishment you ingest or inhale while you sleep, or
fibers that match the quality and characteristics of
Egyptian long staple cotton, are all possible ways to
make the pie bigger.

Trade barriers are not restricted to industry or
agriculture; they are rampant in the service sector as
well.

European Accountants Are Angered by Curbs on
Practicing in the US. ... The EC Commission has
issued under the 1992 program a directive giving
accountants from any EC country the right to

---

[15]W. Edwards Deming, *Out of the Crisis* (Cambridge: MIT CAES,
1986).

practice in another EC nation. A British char-
tered accountant who moves to Germany must
still demonstrate knowledge of German law and
accounting practices by taking a test, but he cannot be denied the right to take the test. This represents a significant breakthrough...[16]

But in the US, six states or territories preclude
foreigners from taking their CPA exam.

All we are asking for in the US is a similar right
as we have won in Europe. ... In many service sec-
tors, the Europeans complain that state regulations are a barrier, that they have to go through
the same process 50 times.[17]

It is no consolation that US accountants must go
through the same process: it only serves to increase
the total cost of doing business, in the long run, and
makes us less competitive. With the advent of cannon,
moats and castle walls lost their effectiveness as
protectors!

Let's imagine for a moment that the barriers
and the walls come down. And let's say that you do become competitive: world-class competitive. What if
you do achieve productivity levels that manufacturers
only dream about today? In fact, Peter Drucker states:

it is highly probable that developed countries such
as the United States or Japan will, by the year

---

[16]"Wall Street Journal," William Echickson, Aug. 21, 1990.
[17]Ibid.

2010, employ no larger a proportion of the labor
force in manufacturing than developed countries
now employ in farming—at most one-tenth.[18]

So what if you do get there? Is this what manufacturing has to look forward to after all of this effort to improve productivity—to be as well off as the farmers? I very definitely think so, unless we are able to balance productivity with quality, timeliness, and greatness.

A standard that can be used to guide improvement in virtually any organization is the **Malcolm Baldrige National Quality Award**. Authorized by Congress in 1987, the Malcolm Baldrige National Quality Award can be won by manufacturing and service businesses of any size. In order to be considered for the award, eligible organizations must submit an Award Examination. Within the Examination guidelines an organization can operationalize the philosophy of Dr. Deming. Here's how.

We must first look at matching the seven Examination Categories with Dr. Deming's Fourteen Points. This is shown if Figure 4.13.

---

[18]Peter F. Drucker, *The Frontiers of Management* (New York: Penguin, 1986).

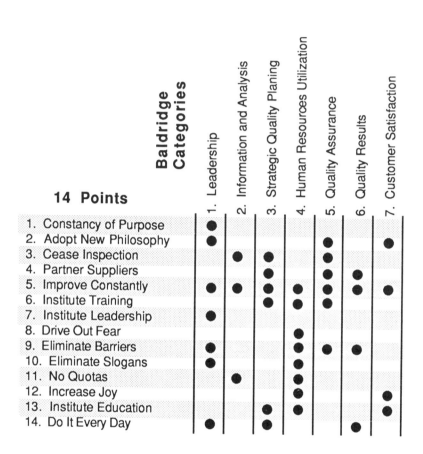

Figure 4.13
Relationships Between Deming's 14 Points
and the 7 Baldrige Categories

Since this section is on **operationalization** of the philosophy of Dr. Deming, I use the 7 categories of the Baldrige Award Criteria[19] to frame this action

Category 1.0   Leadership

1.1 Senior Executive Leadership
1.2 Quality Values
1.3 Management for Quality
1.4 Public Responsibility

Category 2.0   Information and Analysis

2.1 Scope and Management of Quality Data and Information
2.2 Competitive Comparisons and Benchmarks
2.3 Analysis of Quality Data and Information

Category 3.0   Strategic Quality Planning

3.1 Strategic Quality Planning Process
3.2 Quality Goals and Plans

Category 4.0   Human Resource Utilization

4.1 Human Resource Management
4.2 Employee Involvement
4.3 Quality Education and Training
4.4 Employee Recognition and Performance Measurement
4.5 Employee Well-Being and Morale

Category 5.0   Quality Assurance of Products and Services

---

[19]Malcolm Baldrige National Quality Award, 1991 Application Guidelines" NIST, Gaithersburg, 1991.

5.1 Design an Introduction of Quality Products and Services

5.2 Process Quality Control

5.3 Continuous Improvement of Processes

5.4 Quality Assessment

5.5 Documentation

5.6 Business Process and Support Service Quality

5.7 Supplier Quality

Category 6.0 Quality Results

6.1 Product and Service Quality Results

6.2 Business Process, Operational, and Support Service Quality Results

6.3 Supplier Quality Results

Category 7.0 Customer Satisfaction

7.1 Determining Customer Requirements and Expectations

7.2 Customer Relationship Management

7.3 Customer Service Standards

7.4 Commitment to Customers

7.5 Complaint Resolution for Quality Improvement

7.6 Determining Customer Satisfaction

7.7 Customer Satisfaction Results

7.8 Customer Satisfaction Comparison

These seven examination categories are evaluated within three dimensions: approach, deployment, and results. The philosophy of Dr. Deming is the approach method: it is deployed on the physical, logical, and emotional levels; the results speak for themselves.

1.0 Leadership.

Dr. Deming specifically targets leadership as both the source and the downfall of quality. Quality is made in the boardroom. It is vital to describe some attributes of a leader and show how leaders should be selected and developed. By what methods do they lead? They should have developed a Constancy of Purpose Statement that is value oriented. They should balance Quality and Cost over space and time. They should organize for continual improvement and balance that with constancy of purpose.

"Well, as a last ditch measure, we could improve the corporate image by improving the product."[20]

---

[20]Sawyer, "The Wall Street Journal."

In the development of their people, they should balance the individual with the team. All of this should be accomplished on the physical, logical, and emotional levels. I particularly like Laotsu's definition of a leader:

> A leader is best
> When people barely know that he exists,
> Not so good when people obey and acclaim him,
> Worst when they despise him.
> "Fail to honor people, They fail to honor you;"
> But of a good leader, who talks little,
> When his work is done, his aim fulfilled,
> They will all say, "We did this ourselves."[21]

2.0 Information and Analysis.

What is information? You apply a process to collect data and you get an answer. If you apply another process, or apply the same process at a different time, you will get another answer. Before you collect any data, you must first ¿gree on the questions. Dr. Deming tells us that he cannot perform as simple a task as cleaning a table unless he knows how it is going to be used. If you are going to eat off of it, it is clean enough now. If you are going to perform an appendectomy on it, he must use an entirely different process to clean it. If you are going to assemble microchips on it, it may be clean enough for an appendectomy, but not for the assembly of microchips. You cannot determine how to collect the data until you know how it will be used.

---

[21]Laotzu, *The Way of Life*, trans. Witter Brynner. (New York: Perigee Books, 1944).

You should know that some of the more important data are unknown and unknowable. Some of the
known data are quantitative and qualitative. You
should look for positives as well as negatives and use
the PDSA cycle for improvement. You should be striv-
ing to match the Voice of the Customer with the Voice
of the Process. In so doing you will balance listening to
customers, suppliers, competitors, engineers, assemblers, experts, non-experts, and the like. You should
show data over time and display its variability. Remember, the only purpose for collecting data is to take
action, and all actions affect the future.

3.0 Strategic Quality Planning.

Your leaders must be vitally involved in strategic planning because Quality is made in the Boardroom. Your strategy should call for you to cease dependence on mass inspection. It should embrace the
new philosophy: high quality produces high productivity. You should work with your suppliers and customers to break down barriers. You should establish
and expand education and training processes, as they
are vitally necessary for improvement. Your strategic
Planning activities on the macro level should be a part
of an overall PDSA for your business. Examples of
someone else's success or failure are not necessarily
something special for you to copy or avoid. Your strategy should aim to increase the market and deliver Joy
of Ownership through Joy of Workmanship.

4.0 Human Resources Utilization.

The process of fostering Joy of Workmanship will balance the joy that each of us takes as individuals with the joy that each of us takes as a member of a family or team. You need to spend time with your people, considering them as your customers so that you can match their intrinsic needs (Voice of the Customer) with the extrinsic resources that you manage (Voice of the Process). There are a number of sociotechnical tools that you must train everyone to understand and use. You should not break their spirits with meaningless slogans and other barriers. You should lead each of them personally so that they enthusiastically participate in the conduct of the business. Do not create strife and discontent with arbitrary rewards or punishments. You must always balance the performance (good or bad) of the person with the performance of the process. This understanding is essential for leadership.

5.0 Quality Assurance of Products and Services.

You are in a new economic age. You assure quality, not by mass inspection, but by continual improvement of upstream processes. You must have a process to operationally define the Voice of the Customer throughout all areas of your company. This deployment of the Voice of the Customer should balance the letter of the law with the spirit of the law. Quality is made upstream in the Boardroom and design room.

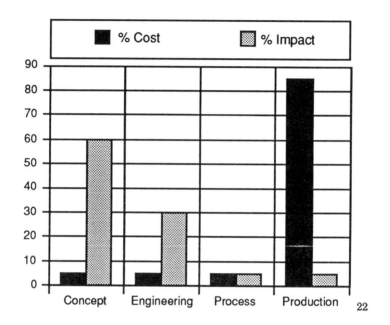

Figure 4.14
A Comparison of the Cost and Impact of Quality

Even though you may spend only 5% of the cost of a program in the Concept phase, you affect about 60% of the total costs spent. You might have the best buggy whip in the world, but no market for it because it is too expensive or the wrong design for the market.

The decisions you make in selecting your suppliers are more important to high quality at a low price than the sophistication of any inspection sampling plan you might devise. It is very convenient for people

---

[22]"A Smart Way to Manufacture," *Business Week,* April 30,1990.

in the quality profession to point to the need for improvement of financial processes or personnel processes. I have found that the quality processes, especially down-stream inspections and audits, contribute more than any other process to short-term thinking, long-term confusion, and the overall deprivation of people's right to take joy in their work. The quality profession itself is in need of major improvement. Everyone must be educated (logical) and trained (physical) and have desire (emotional) to use the PDSA improvement cycle.

6.0 Quality Results.

Results are an important part of the PDSA improvement cycle. They will immediately tell you if your plan or theory does not apply to this world. They also will reinforce your belief that your plan or theory does work to improve the process. No matter what the results, you should show them over time. If there are trends or patterns in the results, this is valuable information for the next iteration of the PDSA improvement cycle. If there are *not* trends or patterns in the results, *this* is valuable information for the next iteration of the PDSA improvement cycle. You should always show the variability of the results. This, along with time ordered data, will help you determine if the variation was a one-time fluke or could be counted on in the future. It is important that you compare the results of other possibly interrelated inputs or outputs. For example, you could jeopardize the profits of the business by encouraging each department to maximize its own profits. I win—we lose. You could also solve one problem, but in the process create another problem for someone else. You must keep all of these tradeoffs visible.

7.0 Customer Satisfaction.

First of all, you want customers who are more than just satisfied. You want them to take Joy in their Ownership of your product or service. This means that you continue to identify and predict the positives as well as the negatives, and appropriately deploy them in your product or service. You should have not only a complaint resolution process but a praise resolution process. These processes must differentiate between special causes and common causes and affect the appropriate action. You should be able to show that you have expanded the market, not just taken a piece of pie away from someone else. Above all, your customers should show increasing Joy of Ownership for a sustained period of time.

A **Common Vocabulary** can reduce confusion. The Navy has a publication entitled "DICNAVAB": Dictionary of Naval Abbreviations. At first, I thought it amusing, but I soon realized that it was vital to the operation of large organizations. Abbreviations, acronyms, and technical terms might be useful in a homogeneous organization, but they can be confusing and wasteful in all other organizations. One of the things that I learned from Jim Bakken at Ford was the necessity to publish a glossary of terms. He realized that people used different words interchangeably. Likewise, the same words meant different things to different people. We were attempting to introduce a blend of science and philosophy that was new to the people at Ford. It was new to anyone. One of the first debates we had was over the definition of Quality. In fact, because of the way that quality had been narrowly defined as inspection of high-volume manufacturing product, I argued that we should not even call what we were doing a part of quality. I lost that argument. We then began to define Quality in a way that expanded it in the view of many people.

In retrospect, I am glad that we did take the time to define it. The definition that we agreed on is neither good nor bad, but it was useful to us as we operationalized it. The definition of Quality that Ford uses is: "Quality is defined by the customer: customers want products and services that, throughout their lives, meet customers' needs and expectations at a cost that represents value."

The **National Cooperative Research Act of 1984** promotes research and development, encourages innovation, stimulates trade, and makes necessary and appropriate modifications in the operation of the antitrust laws. This law physically opens the door for cooperation between organizations so that they can bring together the necessary resources to compete in this new economic age.

For a number of years now, I have told Bill Ouchi's story of his address at an American Trade Association meeting a few winters ago in Miami. I quote from him:

Several months ago, I was a guest speaker at the annual meeting of a U.S. Trade association. The time was late winter, the place was Florida, the audience the 300 or so leaders of companies in the industry. I spoke one morning, after which the conferees adjourned for golf. The next morning they had another speaker, followed by tennis, and the third day another speaker, followed by fishing. Now, don't get me wrong; I am not against golf, tennis, or fishing, nor do I doubt the importance of informal contact in the building of relationships. Nonetheless, I said to my audience that morning: 'While you are out on the golf course this after-noon, waiting for your partner to tee up, I want you to think about something. Last month I was in Tokyo, where I visited your trade association counterpart. It represents the roughly two hun-dred Japanese companies who are your direct competitors. They are now holding meetings from eight each morning until nine each night, five days a week, for three months straight, so that one company's oscilloscope will connect to another company's analyzer, so that they can agree on their needs for changes...and then approach their government with one voice (not two hundred sepa-rate voices each clamoring to be heard) to ask for cooperation. Tell me who you think is going to be in better shape five years from now?[23]

What the Japanese have learned is that no one person, or one company, or one industry, or one sector has enough resources to compete in this new economic age.

---

[23]William Ouchi, *The M-Form Society* (Reading: Addison-Wesley, 1984).

In the United States, we now at last have permission to cooperate in a few of the areas that affect
our competitiveness. The Clayton Act had effectively
prohibited this cooperation. The National Cooperative
Research Act of 1984 goes a long way toward leveling
the ball field. The letter of the law is written. We now
need to understand the intent of the law and operationalize it in the spirit of the law. Physical change
can be swift. Logical and emotional change may take
longer. But in order to compete, we must learn to
cooperate.

> Under a novel agreement with the Holiday Inn
> across the street, the Hecht's store in downtown
> Washington, DC will supplement its sales staff
> with as many as 80 hotel employees during the
> Thanksgiving-to-Christmas shopping rush. The
> holiday season is traditionally slow for any hotel.
> Thus, layoffs and cutbacks from full-time to part-
> time are standard practice during this period, says
> Steve Swantko, marketing director at the hotel.
> "By directing our employees to temporary work at
> Hecht's, we will hopefully be able to retain them
> for when our business picks back up."[24]

In Detroit, there is a new era of cooperation not
in the auto industry, but in the television broadcast
industry. Local stations had been very hesitant to invest money or time on productions that yield only
about an hour on television. But a recent cooperative
effort between the local PBS station, Channel 56, and
the local CBS station, Channel 2, resulted in a record-
breaking 16 Emmy's for each station. The Ravendale

[24]"Insight Magazine," November 20, 1989.

Project which aired simultaneously on both stations was year-long project that was too expensive for any single station's budget. Everyone felt like a winner.

> Everyone came away from the table smiling, and for different reasons. Channel 56's work gets exposure on larger commercial stations; the commercial stations get an association with Channel 56, and the bill is lightened.[25]

A physical list of people that can help you.

There are a number of people who could help you improve. I have developed a list of professionals whom I have recommended to others at Ford and General Motors. This is a dynamic process and I hesitate to formalize it in this book because what is good for General Motors might not be good for you. What follows, however, is my latest letter to the General Managers of General Motors:

OUTSIDE CONSULTING RESOURCES
January 1991

During the past several years, the number of consultants claiming to be experts in Quality has increased dramatically. The sheer magnitude of the numbers and diversity of approaches has made it difficult for a manager to select a competent partner. The situation is all the more critical since the UAW and General Motors have agreed that there will be **one** process for quality and it is to be the Quality Network.

---

[25]"Cooperation Was In the Air at the Emmys," The Detroit News, May 13, 1991.

The list that follows should make the selection process easier because it consists of **people** who have demonstrated, through rigorous screening, approaches to Quality that are consistent with those espoused in the Quality Network.

This is a recommendation for specific individuals, **not** their respective organizations. This is extremely important because of the variability of the quality of personnel within these consulting and educational organizations.

Each individual is categorized either with a **T** to signify capability in the technical aspects of the Quality Network, or a **Q** to signify capability in the philosophical aspects of the Quality Network or a **QN** to signify capability in all aspects of the Quality Network. The QN is not just the sum of a T and a Q but reflects a degree of maturity and profound knowledge that can only be gained through education and experience over a number of years.

The list will be brought up to date in January and July of each year, and is being made available to ensure a consistent approach to Quality at every level of the Company, its supply base, and its network of dealers.

If you are using a Quality consultant not on the list and would like an evaluation, simply contact W. W. Scherkenbach to make the necessary arrangements.

Chapter 5

Logical Change

Dr. Deming states that the **System of Profound Knowledge** appears in four parts, all related to each other:

- Theory of Systems
- Theory of Variation
- Theory of Knowledge
- Theory of Psychology[1]

The application of these four parts spans all three levels of change. Appreciation for a system is physical. The application of statistics and the operationalization of the theory of knowledge is logical. The practice of the theory of psychology is emotional. These interact with each other, corresponding with the Venn diagram in Chapter 3.

---

[1]W. Edwards Deming, Letter: "Need for Change," 3 Oct., 1988.

Theory of Systems

When Dr. Deming uses the word *system*, it is synonymous with the term *process,* as I defined it in Chapter 1. The *aim* of a system, or process, is determined through the operational definition of the Voice of the Customer. The operational definition of any aim or intent is not what you intended it to be, but what resulted when the process was operated.

In this part of Profound Knowledge, I am grateful to my friends Dr. Myron Tribus, Mr. Norbert Keller, Dr. Victor Kane, and Mr. Peter Jessup. All have broadened my perspectives, helping me to improve my knowledge in the Theory of Systems.

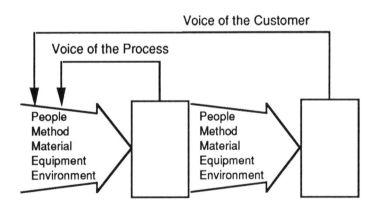

Figure 5.1
Interdependent Processes

We are all part of an interdependent network of processes. And as we already know, it is the job of a leader to optimize the process. Optimization occurs over space and time, and while leaders strive toward optimization, it can never be completely achieved. There is always one more factor—Person, Material, Method, Equipment, or Environment—which can be included within the process boundaries. And there is always the next period of time that can be included. But even though optimization can never be achieved, it is always an aim and a limit.

Social Memory, defined as the group memory of past experiences, is necessary for optimization of a process. Without it there can be no differentiation of *special* from *common* causes of variation: every cause will be seen as special. Social Memory also facilitates the actions that will bring joy as part of the team, rather than as an individual. People know that they will find joy as individuals at some time in the future. This sequence of sacrifice can also be reversed. It is a balance of space (individual vs team) and time (short-term vs long-term). We suboptimize because it makes sense, given our current knowledge of the world. But it is costly as this example describes.

How to be Efficient With Fewer Violins

For considerable periods of time the four oboe players had nothing to do. The number should be reduced and the work spread more evenly over the whole of the concert, thus eliminating peaks of activity.

All 12 violins were playing identical notes; this seems unnecessary duplication. The staff of this section should be drastically cut. If a larger volume of sound is required, it would be obtained by means of electronic apparatus.

Much effort was absorbed in the playing of sixteenth, eighth and quarter notes; this seems to be an unnecessary refinement. It is recommended that all notes be rounded up to the nearest quarter. If this were done it would be possible to use trainees and lower grade operatives more extensively...

Obsolescence of equipment is another matter into which further investigation should be made, as it was reputed in the program that the leading violinist's instrument was already several hundred years old. If normal depreciation schedules had been applied the value of this instrument should have been reduced to zero.

There seems to be too much repetition of some musical passages. Scores should be drastically pruned. No useful purpose is served by repeating on the horns a passage which has already been handled by the strings. It is estimated that if all the redundant passages were eliminated the whole concert time of two hours could be reduced to 20 minutes, and there would be no need for an intermission.[2]

Suboptimization is everywhere. In one company, the Facilities Management Department routinely turns off the air-conditioning on evenings and weekends, even though many people must work during that time. Computer equipment is also affected by the heat. Facilities Management saves money and meets

---

[2]Source could not be found. A *similar* passage was found in R. M. Fulmer and T. T. Herbert, *Exploring the New Management* (New York: MacMillian, 1974), p.27.

their budget, but the rest of the company loses.[3] Dr. Deming tells many examples of a person or a department "winning" while the rest of the company "loses."

I frequently use a modified "Red-Blue" or "Prisoners' Dilemma" or "Win All You Can" exercise[4] in my own 1–day course: "Introduction to the Philosophy of Dr. Deming." The aim of the exercise is to show the participants that a balance of individual work and team-work is necessary for prosperity. If the audience is primarily from Western cultures, I change the scoring to emphasize the need for teamwork. If the audience is primarily from Eastern cultures, I change the scoring to emphasize the need for individual expression. The exercise consists of:

People: Manager
4 departments of at least two
people each

Material: 4 pads of scratch paper
Viewgraphs of monthly, quarterly,
and annual reports

Equipment: 4 pencils
Overhead projector,
and screen

Environment: Pressure to perform.

Method: See flow diagram.

---

[3]Contributed by Stuart Moulder

[4]For a good exposition on these exercises, read Chapter 15 of *The Deming Dimension* by Henry Neave (Knoxville: SPC Press, Inc., 1990).

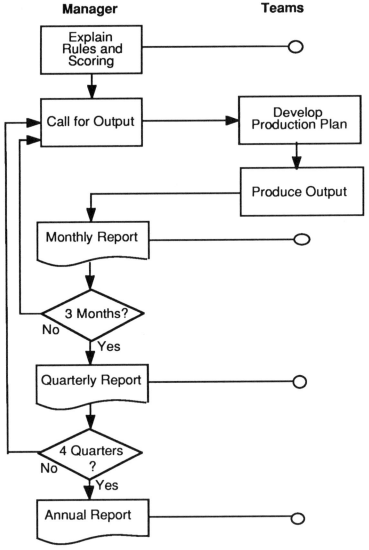

Figure 5.2
Flow Diagram for "Win All You Can"

Figure 5.2 outlines the procedure and Figure 5.3 demonstrates the scoring rules that I use to balance teamwork with individual achievement. To make the exercise emulate Western culture, I double the next month's score of the team with the highest quarterly results; I also acknowledge them as the "Department of the Quarter" (see Figure 5.4). For example, if Department C has the highest score for the first quarter, their April score is doubled. I urge the departments to put company interests first. If each department, in a spirit of teamwork, produced y's, the company would gain 60 points. If each, trying to increase the departmental scores, produced x's, the company would also gain 60 points. If the departments cooperated and balanced individual and team accomplishments, the company would gain 180 points. Any other strategy loses points for the company.

Scoring Rules

Production		Score	
		X's	Y's
4 x's	0 y's	1	0
3 x's	1 y	−2	−1
2 x's	2 y's	3	3
1 x	3 y's	−1	−2
0 x's	4 y's	0	1

Figure 5.3
Scoring Rules for "Win All You Can"

Month	Dept. A	Dept.B	Dept. C	Dept. D
January				
February				
March				
1st Quarter				

Figure 5.4
Chart of Scores for "Win All You Can"

Theory of Variation

There is a critical shortage of leaders today who understand the theory of variation. Dr. Deming describes what knowledge this entails:

- Some understanding of variation;
- Understanding of the capability of a process;
- That leadership of people is entirely different in the two states: stable and unstable;
- Knowledge about the different kinds of uncertainty in statistical data;
- That there are two mistakes in attempts to improve a process;
- Knowledge of procedures aimed at minimum economic loss;
- Knowledge about interaction of forces;
- Understanding of the distinction between enumerative studies and analytic problems;
- Knowledge about the losses that come from unfortunate successive application of random forces that may, individually, be unimportant.

Some of the people whom I find to have a very helpful understanding of variation include my professional colleagues, Dr. Donald Wheeler, Dr. Gipsie Ranney, Dr. Brian Joiner, and Dr. Richard DeVor.

One of the aims of Chapter 1 was to give you some understanding of variation in processes. It is everywhere. You can hear it in the Voice of the Customer. You can hear it in the Voice of the Process.

When the Voice of the Process is stable over a period of time, as shown in Figure 5.5, it builds your degree of belief that if you could keep the same blend of People, Material, Method, Equipment, and Environment, you should expect to see the same pattern of outcomes.

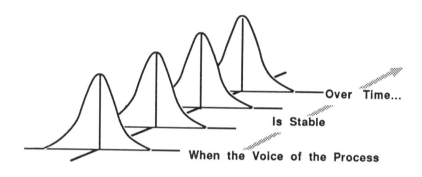

Figure 5.5
A Stable Process Over Time

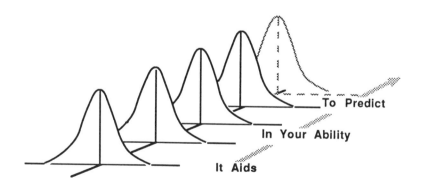

Figure 5.6
Statistical Stability and Prediction

You make decisions that affect the future. If the data indicate that the process on which you must act is stable, then your chance to affect the future as expected, is better than if the process was not stable. You can add to your knowledge of the subject matter with statistical stability.

On the other hand, if the data indicate that the process is not stable, then your prediction of the future is based on your previous knowledge of the subject matter. Also, your degree of belief in that subject matter should be diminished because of the lack of stability of the recent data (see Figure 5.7).

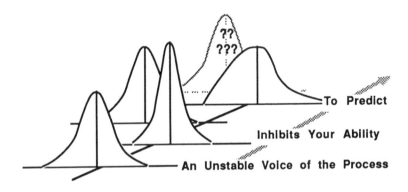

Figure 5.7
Process Instability and Prediction

Of course, you could always guess what will happen in the future. That is how we often project the Voice of the Customer.

"A projection is a guess
wrapped in a nice binder." [5]

But the Voice of the Customer, like the Voice of the Process, varies over time. It also varies from customer to customer.

When it is stable over a period of time, as in Figures 5.8 and 5.9, it builds your degree of belief that the needs and expectations of your customers, as you have translated them, will maintain the same pattern in the future.

---

[5]"Selling Short," Ross and Raden, Universal Press Syndicate, 1987.

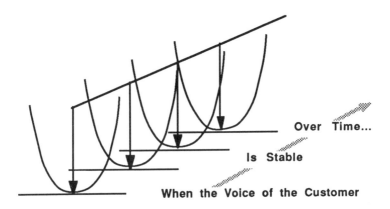

Figure 5.8
Stability in the Voice of the Customer

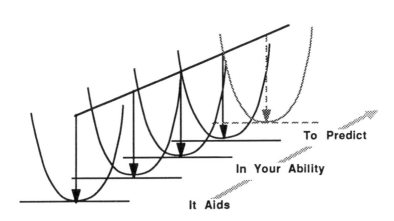

Figure 5.9
Customer Stability and Prediction

If the Voice of the Customer is not stable over a period of time, as in Figure 5.10, then your prediction of the future needs and expectations of your customers is based on your previous translations. Also, your degree of belief in those translations should be diminished because of the lack of stability of the recent data.

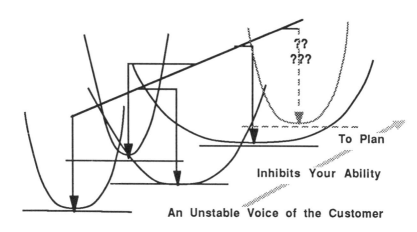

Figure 5.10
An Unstable Voice of the Customer

The **capability** of a process is the same as "the Gap" which I presented in Chapter 3. It is estimated by the comparison of a **stable** Voice of the Process with a **stable** Voice of the Customer (Figure 5.11).

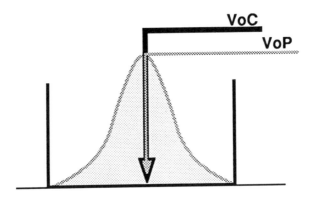

Figure 5.11
A Stable Voice of Process Compared to
A Stable Voice of Customer

If either the Voice of the Customer or the Voice of the Process is unstable, there is no capability of a process. You may do calculations, but they are meaningless with respect to the future of the relationship with your customers. If the Voice of the Customer is stable but the process is not stable, the ability of the process to consistently match the customer requirements is in doubt (Figure 5.12). This view of capability should be very familiar to those in manufacturing. Specifications are from the Voice of the Customer, while the 6 sigma spread of the process is from the Voice of the Process. Specifications for the product change far less often than the output of the process.

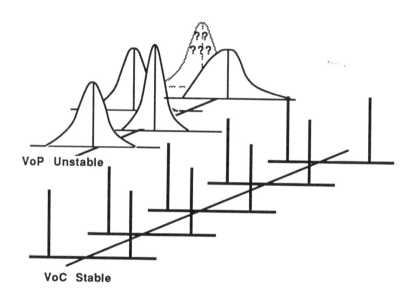

Figure 5.12
Results of an Unstable Voice of Process on Predictability

If the Voice of the Process is stable but the requirements of your customers are not stable, process capability is meaningless with respect to the changing

Voice of the Customer (Figure 5.13). The ability of a plant to meet production schedules is a good example of this situation. The quantity and mix of product required in any time period by the sales and distribution process can change far more rapidly than the output of the production process.

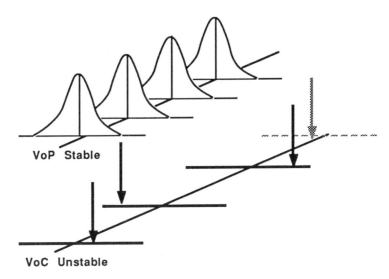

VoP Stable

VoC Unstable

Figure 5.13
Results of an Unstable Voice of Customer on Predictability

You will see in Chapter 6 some examples of stable and unstable forecasts which are usually not visible in reports to management.

Process capability is information for the future. Should you adopt process A instead of process B? Should you go after customer niche C in addition to customer niche D? Should you do business with supplier E instead of supplier F or G? To what degree should you trust person H? What degree of belief can be placed in measurement process I? What should your inventory be to meet sales forecast J? All of these decisions depend on the capability of the process. All of these decisions depend on the stability of the Voice of the Customer and the Voice of the Process. All of these decisions can be aided by knowledge of statistical theory.

The aim of any statistical study must be to provide you with a basis for action. Not just any action, but action appropriate to the improvement of the process. Much of the theory of statistics that you have learned and will learn is useful for what Dr. Deming calls **enumerative** studies, where the action is taken on what was studied. Unfortunately, most of the decisions that you as a process manager must make are in the domain of what Dr. Deming calls **analytic** studies, where the action is taken on what produced what was studied. The distinction between the two studies depends on your perspective. The process model in Figure 5.14 will help to illustrate this.

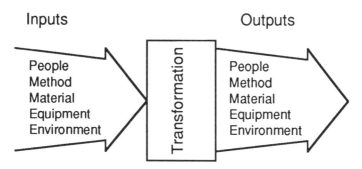

Figure 5.14
Inputs and Outputs of A Process

Action in an enumerative study is on the People, Materials, Methods, Equipment, and Environment which are outcomes of the process. Its aim is to count, describe, or evaluate some output of a process. You have produced 1000 engines today and you would like to evaluate their quality. Hurricane Hugo has just struck and you wish to count the number of homes that were washed away. The quarter has just closed and you wish to estimate the value of inventory on hand. All of these are in the domain of enumerative methods. The action is taken on the outcomes (Figure 5.15).

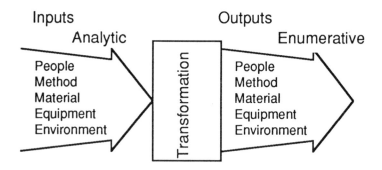

Figure 5.15
Action in Analytic and Enumerative Studies

Action in an analytic study, is on the People, Materials, Methods, Equipment, and Environment that will produce the outcomes for future enumerative studies. In other words, action is on the inputs to a process. You would like to improve the process that will produce the next 1000 engines. You desire to prevent the damage from the next hurricane, or to reduce the amount of inventory on hand next quarter. All of these are in the domain of analytic methods. The action is taken on the upstream process that will produce the outcomes. But as one person's outcomes are another person's inputs, one person's enumerative study may be another person's analytic study (Figure 5.16).

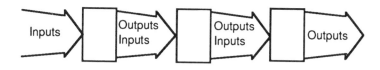

Figure 5.16
Interdependence of Outputs and Inputs

Every decision you make is under conditions of uncertainty. Change continually occurs over space and time. You will always have erroneous, ambiguous, and confusing information about the past, present, or future. Under some conditions, statistical methods can help you to describe the bounds of uncertainty of past data, thus helping you take appropriate actions to reduce uncertainty. The more we know about the uncertainties or limitations of the data, the more useful they become to us as we act on them.

There are 2 types of uncertainty in enumerative studies: uncertainties due to statistical sampling and uncertainties due to the equal complete coverage (Figure 5.17). The total uncertainty in an enumerative study is a combination of the statistical and non-statistical errors.

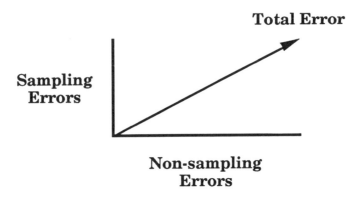

Total Error

Sampling Errors

Non-sampling Errors

Figure 5.17
Two Types of Uncertainty in Enumerative Studies

When non-sampling errors are large, it is uneconomical and ineffective to waste funds on a big sample. While a big sample will decrease the *sampling* error, it leaves the *total* error about the same.

> One must face the fact that the overall usefulness and reliability of a survey may actually be enhanced by cutting down on the size of the sample and using the money saved to reduce the non-sampling errors.[6]

---

[6] W. Edwards Deming, *Sample Design in Business Research* (New York: John Wiley & Sons, 1960).

There are sampling and non-sampling errors in an analytic study too. But they are dynamic. They vary over time with each enumerative snapshot of the process (see Figure 5.18).

These errors are not additive, but their pattern over time influences your degree of belief in your knowledge of the process. If the pattern of errors is stable, as it is in Dr. Deming's studies of the transportation industry, then you may quantify the uncertainties of the study. If they are not stable because of varying sample sizes, different sampling plans, surveys, measurements, process changes, or the like, then you may not quantify the uncertainty of the study. Like capability, you may perform the calculations, but they are meaningless.

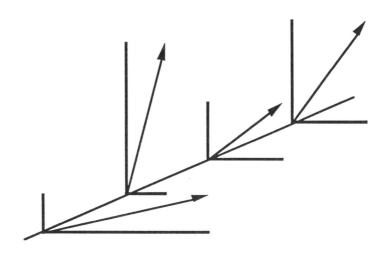

Figure 5.18
Errors in Analytic Studies

The uncertainties in data can contribute to inappropriate actions to improve the process. If you think that the process with all of its uncertainties is stable, or in statistical control, you would take some specific action to improve the process. That action would be directed on the People, Material, Method, Equipment, or Environment that contribute to common causes of variation in the process. If the process turned out to be unstable, the action that you took would be less efficient and less effective than if you had recognized the instability. For example, if you thought that the cause for late engineering designs was common to all departments and that they could do something about it, you might issue a letter to all of them telling them to take action. If the cause for the late designs was actually special to one of the departments, your letter might have caused changes in other departments that were, in effect, "moving the funnel."

Conversely, if you think that the process is unstable, you would focus your action to remove or enhance the specific People, Material, Method, Equipment, or Environment that specially caused the instability. If the process turned out to be stable, the action you took would be less efficient and less effective than if you had recognized the stability. For example, if a project has a large negative gap between the the target, and the actual for the ROI, you might reassign the project manager. If the cause for the low ROI was due to a senior executive committee that tampered with every project, then the fear caused by the reassignment could result in a very risk-aversive organization.

Dr. Walter Shewhart of the Bell Telephone Laboratories first made the distinction between controlled and uncontrolled variation, due to what we call common and special causes, while studying process data in the 1920's. He developed a simple but powerful tool to dynamically separate the two—he developed the control chart. *There is empirical evidence that control charts effectively direct attention toward special causes of variation when they appear and reflect the extent of common cause variation that must be reduced by the action of management.*[7] The aim of control charts is to minimize the economic loss caused by confusion of special causes and common causes. You can always act on every piece of data as if it was a special cause, but you would incur the losses of tampering. The rules of the funnel apply here—off you go to the Milky Way! You can always treat every piece of data as though it was a common cause, but you would miss cheap and quick opportunities for improvement.

Special causes of variation can be detected by simple statistical methods. These causes of variation are not common to all People, Material, Method, Equipment, and Environment in the process. The discovery of a special cause, and its removal or its incorporation, are usually the responsibility of the manager of the local process. Remember, we all are managers of processes. Sometimes, however, other managers in the interdependent network of processes are in a better position to take action on the special cause.

---

[7]Pete Jessup, *Continuing Process Control and Process Capability Improvement* (Dearborn: The Ford Motor Company, 1984).

The extent of **common causes** of variation can be shown by simple statistical methods, but the causes themselves need other statistical methods to isolate them. These common causes of variation are usually the responsibility of other managers in the interdependent network of processes. Sometimes, however, the manager of the local process is in a better position to identify these causes and pass the information on to other managers for action.

A Theory of Knowledge

Not many people have studied a **theory of knowledge**. And yet, epistemology should have been your most important course in school or in life. Like any subject matter, there is more than one theory of knowledge. In this part, I do defer to several friends from whom I have learned much: Dr. Howard Kisner, Dr. Peter Koestenbaum, and of course, Dr. Deming. Some theories are more useful than others. They range from the assumption that all knowledge is a priori, to the idea that all knowledge is empirical. Dr. Deming has chosen to highlight the essentials that apply to most epistemologies:

- Any rational plan requires prediction.
- Interpretation of data from a test or experiment is prediction.
- A statement devoid of prediction conveys no knowledge.

- Theory leads to questions. Without questions, experience and examples teach nothing.

- Communication and negotiation require, for optimization, operational definitions.

- No number of examples establishes a theory.

- There is no true value of any characteristic, state, or condition that is defined in terms of measurement or observation.

- There is no such thing as a *fact*, concerning empirical observation.

Dr. Deming has been greatly influenced by C.I. Lewis. In particular, his *Mind and the World Order* is the basis for most of the bullet points above.[8]

What follows are my views of each of the points that Dr. Deming chose to highlight, although they are not in the order that he used. My words here are purposely those of a layman. My words here should simplify the subject matter and yet keep the subtleties that the experts will recognize. My intent is not to overburden you with technical jargon and overly complex statements, but to provide a useful summation of the ideas. This subject, even more than statistics, has been squandered by obtuse terminology from patronizing professionals.

---

[8]C.I. Lewis, *The Mind and World Order* (New York: Dover Publications, 1929).

Before we begin, I think it appropriate to keep in mind one of the few useful quotations from Arthur Schopenhauer:

> It is dangerous to read about a subject before we have thought about it ourselves. ... When we read, another person thinks for us; we merely repeat his mental process. ... So it comes about that if anyone spends almost the whole day in reading, ... he gradually loses the capacity for thinking...[9]

Perhaps I should have put this quote at the end of the book, but I placed it here to urge you to think. None of this is "instant pudding." You cannot delegate learning. You cannot delegate your own improvement.

Why should you be concerned with a theory of knowledge? Why not just have an "epistemologist" on your staff to complement your financial, engineering, legal, and quality experts? There is no one answer I can give you since others have probably failed for years to convince you and your predecessors. I do know that you need a specific blend of Physical, Logical, and Emotional cues for your transformation.

There is an increasing number of experts in economics, management, political science, and social science who recognize the importance of knowledge in this new economic age. Dr. Deming, Peter Drucker,

---

[9]Arthur Schopenhauer, *Parerga and Paralipomena* (Oxford: Oxford University Press, 1934).

Donald Petersen, Robert Reich, Alvin Toffler, and others see important trends in the Voice of the Customer and have prescribed plans that accelerate the improvement of the knowledge necessary to move the Voice of the Process.

Dr. Deming has said many times that we "know" a lot that just isn't so. The costs of our supposed "knowledge" are buried in the waste, rework, lost sales, complex procedures, and suboptimzed systems. For everyone to learn, everyone must learn how to learn. The process model should serve as our guide for any theory of knowledge. I categorize all theories as Methods in the process model. A theory of knowledge is implied in the Plan-Do-Study-Act Cycle, or the Method for Continual Improvement.

First, we must define our vocabulary. Notice that I did not say *operationally* define, because that requires agreement between customers and suppliers. These are the definitions as I see them.

• **Experience** is a Physical, Logical, or Emotional event that directly involved you. If you are willing to be more adventurous or less skeptical than Descartes, you can widen the definition of experience to include events which indirectly involved you. Indirect events include those that you have read about, or were told about by others who have experienced them.

10

- **Theory** is taken from the Greek $\theta\varepsilon\alpha$—to view or contemplate. In broad terms, a theory is a conceptual explanation of a specific combination of People, Material, Method, Equipment, and Environment. This includes process combinations that link with your experiences, and combinations that are pure Method, such as mathematics, some geometries, and deductive reasoning. The first question that you know, *a priori*, is "What was that?" (even though you ask it after the fact). All other questions come from other theory.

     And theory will affect your subsequent experiences. A statistician, a philosopher, and a CEO went

---

[10]"Ziggy," Universal Press Syndicate, 1988.

on a study mission to Japan. They went together to the same places, but they "saw" quite different things. The statistician "saw" statistical methods; the philosopher "saw" the esthetic impact of Zen; the CEO "saw" policies executed with precision. Each had a different theory, thus each had different questions and different experiences.

• **Knowledge** is theory that you apply over time. Knowledge of Physical, Logical, and Emotional experiences requires the anticipation of future experiences or the remembrance of past experiences. Knowledge may be empirical in that it is never completely verified: it is always under the test of the next experience. It is limited by space and time. The Voice of the Process may not match the Voice of the Customer the next time around, or the next customer around. Empirical knowledge is also gained when theory is not verified over time. Then you have knowledge of what is not useful in a given space or time. Knowledge may also be conceptual, in that it does not depend on empirical verification for its usefulness. Mathematical theorems, logic, and geometric theorems are examples of conceptual knowledge. It is limited only by space: time is of no concern here.

• **Wisdom** is the application of knowledge through philosophy. It requires a long-term perspective that transcends your mortality. Unfortunately, "Wisdom is rare."[11] The Confucianist view of wisdom

---

[11]Inscription dated 1870 on a wall in the Blackfriars Pub, London, England.

is to speak first and then act accordingly. Wisdom is the correspondence of words with actions. A person with big words and little actions has little wisdom. Likewise, a person with little words and big actions has little wisdom. The Voice of the Process must match the Voice of the Customer to have great wisdom.

Dr. Deming has said many times that management's job is prediction. This is because prediction increases knowledge, and knowledge is a prerequisite for action. When the predictions and the actions coincide, this increases wisdom. In order to predict, you must have data. To collect data, you must first ask a question. To ask a question, you must first have a theory. This is why I see the Plan-Do-Study-Act-Cycle as a theory of knowledge (Figure 5.19).

Figure 5.19
The Plan-Do-Study-Act Cycle:
A Theory of Knowledge

A **theory of knowledge** is my conceptual explanation of how a specific combination of People, Material, Method, Equipment, and Environment will repeatedly produce, or not produce, some predicted change in those People, Material, Method, Equipment, and Environment. Bud Chicoine, when he was Vice President for Purchasing at Ford, commented to Dr. Deming and me, "I know what I told our buyers; I do not know what they heard." Rod McKuen wrote "If you had listened hard enough, you might have heard what I meant to say."[12] So I will say it again, but with different words. I think that many philosophers agree that knowledge consists of percepts, concepts, and emotives, as well as theory and time, although, they might use different language, or view it from a different perspective.

Percepts are of your personal world (Figure 5.20). The R-complex plays a major role in their formation. They are what you feel, taste, see, hear, and smell. They are qualitative and subjective. They are part of your world of experiences. You do not see the same color of blue in the sky that I see. We may agree to call a certain wavelength of light "blue." We may agree to look at a specific location in the sky with a certain procedure, but the blue that you see is different than the blue that I see.

We may agree on a process for interviewing applicants for a job, but your view of the people is different than my view. We may both attend the same seminar, but what you hear is different than what I hear.

---

[12]Rod McKuen, "TimePiece" from *Beyond the Board-walk* (Hollywood: Cheval Books, 1972).

The fear that you feel is different from the fear that I feel. The question is, how much different are our percepts? This depends on the links between percepts, concepts, and emotives.

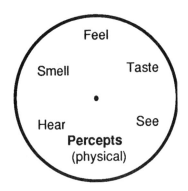

Figure 5.20
Personal Physical Percepts

Concepts are of the mind. The neo-cortex plays a major role in their formation. Concepts are ineffable, but they are definable in the sense that you can describe a particular example of a concept which you have in your mind. What I am attempting to do in this book is to describe, through particulars, some of my concepts of Dr. Deming's philosophy. One of the purposes of a dictionary is to describe concepts. The logical linkage of concepts is theory. Remember, the definition that I gave for theory is a conceptual explanation of a specific combination of People, Material, Method, Equipment, and Environment.

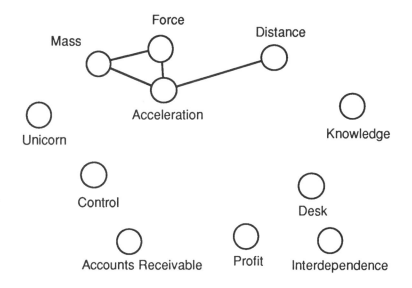

Figure 5.21
Concepts and Linkage of Concepts

No concept or linkage of concepts (theory), is wrong, but some are more useful than others in this world. Concepts may make full, partial, or no contact with this world.

Emotives are also of the mind (illustrated in Figure 5.22) . The Limbic system plays a major role in their formation. Emotives can be logically linked with their opposite: i.e., anxiety with courage, fear with security, misery with joy, and even pride with pride. One of the reasons that Dr. Deming stopped using the term "pride of workmanship" was because of the double-edged meaning of the word pride. Turn up the gain on just about any virtue and you get a vice. Emotives may also make only partial or no contact with your percepts and concepts of this world.

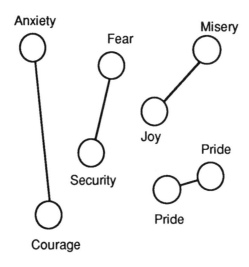

Figure 5.22
Emotives

Now let's put it all together. Figure 5.23 is a major modification of, and an improvement on, the model that appears in *Einstein's Space and Van Gogh's Sky* by Leshan and Margenau.[13] The major components of this graphic are Percepts, Concepts, and Emotives.

---

[13]Leshan and Margenau, *Einstein's Space and Van Gogh's Sky* (New York: Collier Books, 1982).

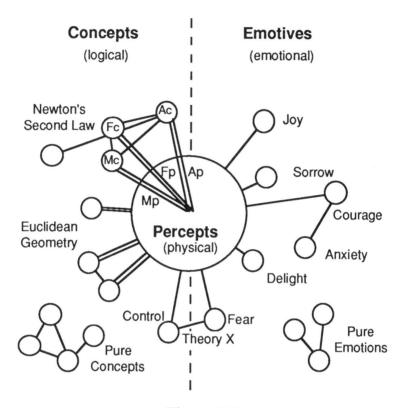

Figure 5.23
A Graphic View of a Theory of Knowledge

I myself can feel (percept) force, mass, and ac-celeration in this world. There are also a number of ways in which I can define them conceptually, as well as logically link them together. One logical linkage theorizes that F= ma. The double lines that link per-ceptual force (Fp) with conceptual force (Fc) are an indication that we have operationally defined Force. In other words, we have linked a specific conceptual definition with a specific percept through a specific process. The definition that we agreed on is neither correct nor incorrect, but is useful for our purpose. Operational definitions serve to reduce the difference between my perceptions and the actions they lead me to take, and your perceptions and the actions that you take. The double lines to the center of this perceptual world indicate that I believe them to be useful everywhere; throughout all space.

The double lines that link the concepts of Euclidean geometry to this world, stop at the surface to indicate that they are only partly useful in this world. Specifically, they are useful over small distances where a flat plane can be approximated. Over larger distances, Euclidian geometry does not apply, but spherical, Riemannian, or other geometries might apply. The theory of Euclidian geometry, like any theory, is correct. Its usefulness in this world, however, is limited. The single lines that connect the concepts and emotives of McGregor's Theory X[14] to this world indicate that they have only been conceptually defined and are only useful in a portion of this world.

Knowledge requires a temporal spread. You may experience a concept in isolation; you may experience an emotive in isolation; you may experience a percept in isolation, but, "...there is no knowledge of external reality without the anticipation of future experience."[15] If your percepts, concepts, and emotives are stable over time, you have knowledge.

---

[14] D.N. McGregor, *The Human Side of Enterprise* (New York: McGraw Hill, 1960).

[15] C.I. Lewis, *Mind and the World Order* (New York: Dover Publications, 1929).

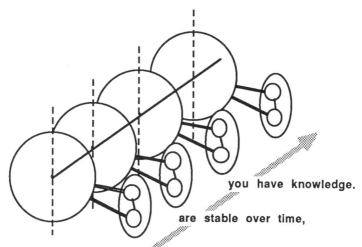

you have knowledge.

are stable over time,

If your Percepts, Concepts and Emotives

Figure 5.24
Knowledge Requires Temporal Spread

C. I. Lewis writes:

Knowledge has two opposites, ignorance and error. If I can observe things from every angle, the restriction to one perspective at a time will not mean necessary ignorance. ... But if perception were restricted to a single angle, that relativity would mean ignorance. ... Ignorance of whatever sort increases the likelihood of error.[16]

---

[16] C.I. Lewis, *Mind and the World Order* (New York: Dover Publications, 1929).

I think that Dr. William Ouchi's "superstitious learning"[17] is a form of ignorance. It occurs when some concepts or emotives are singularly linked with percepts. If you only have one perspective, you might be convinced that your world is round. You look at it today and it is round. You look at it tomorrow and it is round. Past generations that were limited to the same perspective also said that it was round.

For years, managers were positive that the only way to get people to work was to closely control them and keep them indebted to the organization. The concept of control and the emotive of fear were singularly linked to the behavior of the workers. Theory X prospered (shown in Figure 5.25).

But if you link your percepts to different concepts, you can, in effect, change your perspective. Your interpretation of what you experience might be different. You might see that your world is not always round. You might see that people do not need close control and fear to perform effectively. The concept of self control and the emotive of self-satisfaction can also explain the percepts. Theory Y gained acceptance (see Figure 5.26).

---

[17]William Ouchi, *The M-Form Society* (Reading: Addison-Wesley, 1984).

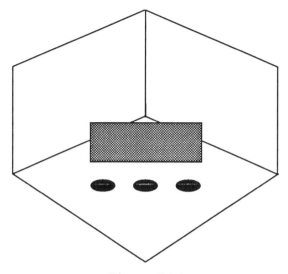

Figure 5.25
Theory X

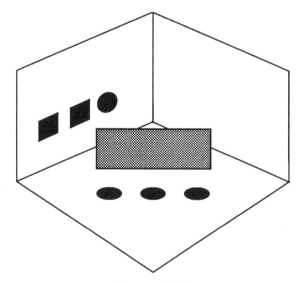

Figure 5.26
Theory Y

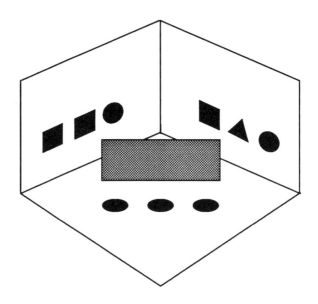

Figure 5.27
Theory Z

Yet another perspective is gained by Theory Z. The concept of subtlety and the emotive of trust[18] add another explanation of the performance of people. Theory X alone, or Theory Y alone, or Theory Z alone are examples of superstitious learning because each is limited to a single perspective. You need all three perspectives and even more if you are to improve your knowledge.

---

[18]William Ouchi, *Theory Z* (New York: Avon Books, 1981).

No theory is right or wrong; each can give you a perspective of this world or others. Some perspectives, however, are more useful than others. You must strive to expand your perspectives. Dr. Deming often asks the same question to different people. Each answer increases the number of perspectives on whatever he wishes to improve. One could also ask different questions of the same person, in order to increase the number of perspectives. The different questions may come from the same theory or different theories. The increase of perspectives is a key to the reduction of ignorance, or superstitious learning, or "knowing a lot that is not so."

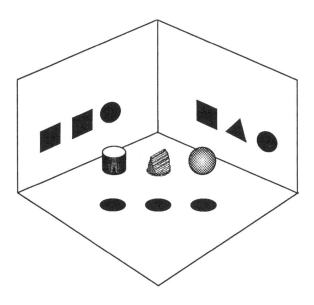

Figure 5.28
You'll Never Have Complete Information

Percy Bridgman wrote:

> I observe that as I get older my attitude changes in a way which I think is significant. When I was younger I had a certain facility in reading a formal logical analysis, which I could do with satisfaction and with conviction that everything was in order. But as I get older I lose my sense of ease in the operations of logic. I do not think this loss is due to senile decay, but I believe that it is rather because I now see more than I did before.[19]

Unfortunately, you will never be able to "remove the curtain" to see all of the perspectives of what it is that you wish to explain.

I think it is folly to try to put a probability on the usefulness of empirical knowledge. A number can be calculated by dividing the number of verifications of the theory by the total number of trials. But the number so obtained is not useful. You may have a million verifications of the theory. But if the next test is inexplicably contrary to the first million, it casts a pall over the usefulness of the theory in this world at this time. The probability number will change imperceptibly, but it may influence the scientist to look to different theory. If you are not concerned about the usefulness of the theory in this world, then you do not need any examples to verify it. If your theory connects pure concepts, there also is no need for examples of verification.

---

[19] Percy Bridgman, *Reflections of a Physicist* (New York: Philosophical Library, 1955).

The latest theories on the processes of our brain seem to mirror on this micro-process level the methods we commonly use on a more macro-process level. Alan Gevins, director of EEG Systems Laboratory, states:

> Our brains seem to devote a very large portion of their activity to continuously forming, maintaining, and revising detailed simulations, or models, of what we imagine our self- and world-states to be... What we experience as "thought" may actually be the brain revising its models to accommodate new information.[20]

I think that we should not, and in fact, do not react to all new information as if it were a special cause for action. We are not single-celled animals who react to every contact with our world. We are multicelled animals who can discriminate between a myriad of experiences and those that cause appropriate action. We continuously reentrain our world in a relative, Voice of the Process-like way. We continuously say, "I've seen this before; I don't need to take any special action." Or we say, "I've never seen this before; I do need to take special action."

Ford Motor Company, like many major corporations, has a leadership course for senior executives. It is a week long and its aim is to strengthen the bonds between members of the worldwide executive team. When I attended in 1986, we stayed the first night at

---

[20]Rick Weiss, "Shadows of Thoughts Revealed," *Science News*, 10 Nov. 1990,© 1990 by Science Services. (Used by permission).

Greenfield Village where we were immersed in the roots and history of the company. We spent the rest of the week building on that history and planning for the future. We covered every aspect of the business, looking at strategies as well as tactics. All of this is what you would expect from a business course.

But on the morning of the last day, Dr. Peter Koestenbaum of San Jose State University prepared the class for their meeting in the afternoon with either Don Petersen or "Red" Poling. It is the meeting with Dr. Koestenbaum that people remember because it was the highlight of the week. Koestenbaum's expertise is not finance, or strategic planning, or quality, or any of the other functions that make up a business. Dr. Koestenbaum is a philosopher. And the chord that he struck in each of the very pragmatic, technically competent business people, affects us to this day. Dr. Koestenbaum was a student of C.I. Lewis, who greatly influenced Dr. Deming and Dr. Shewhart, and he provided the Ford executives with another perspective on what Dr. Deming was teaching them.

Operational Definitions

Operational definitions help to link what I see with what you see. They are a vital part of the linkage between the Voice of the Customer and the Voice of the Process. When the producer does not realize the intent of the customer, there will probably be a gap.

The annual kids' party at Northville Swim
Club last week ended a half-hour earlier than
scheduled. The planned water "wrestle" with a
greased watermelon (which was to conclude the
games) had to be abandoned after one of the assisting mothers, not realizing the intended use for
the green melon, thought she was helping when
she sliced it.[21]

The gaps in industry are far greater than the
one at the Northville Swim Club. There is untold
waste resulting from strict attention to the letter of the
law, while misunderstanding the intent of that law, or
not buying into the spirit of the law. Operational definitions help prevent the rework that is built into our
ways of doing business.

The aim of Policy Deployment, or Quality Function Deployment, or Cascading Communication is the
operational definition of the Voice of the Customer.
One example that Dr. Deming uses to help us see the
usefulness of operational definitions involves a wool
blanket. A customer wishes to buy a blanket that is
50% wool. He has a concept of what 50% wool is. A
producer translates what he perceives to be the Voice
of the Customer into specifications to make a blanket
that is 50% wool. It seems simple enough, but there
can be a large gap between what the customer meant
by 50% wool and what the producer though he meant
by 50% wool.

---

[21]"The Northville Record," August 6, 1986.

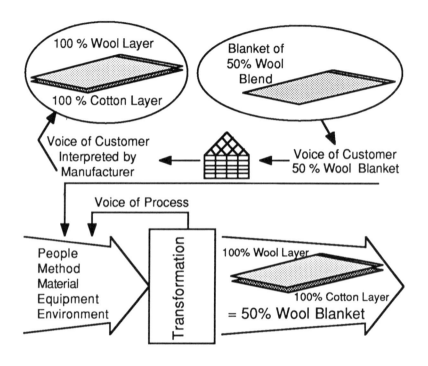

Figure 5.29
Misinterpreting the Voice of the Customer

The customer's concept was that the wool would be dispersed within the blanket in a certain way. The producer translated that to mean that if the top half was all wool and the bottom half was all cotton, the blanket would meet the customer's requirements. The blanket met the internal specifications of the producer, but those specifications had no contact with the world of the customer.

From this example, you can easily see why an organization can go out of business even when they make all of their product according to their specifications. John Guaspari tells an entertaining story about just such an organization in his book *I Know It When I See It.*[22]

Dr. Deming says that quality is made at the top. Operations can do no better than the intent of those in top management. This is necessary but not sufficient. Unfortunately, the operational definition of any intent is what you get when you operationalize it. The intent of management might have been to give the customer a wool blanket that was useful to him. But if management does not have a process that can operationally define their intent, then they have not diminished their risk of going out of business.

The intent of a particular group of top managers is to provide their people with all of the resources necessary to prosper. They are at the stage in the development of the product where they are talking to a focus group of potential customers about the intended color (blue). The team then works to operationally define the shade of blue to the point of precise specifications for the operations. The Voice of the Customer is thus translated. Management then invests in a process that should consistently meet the Voice of the Customer. And in fact it does. The product is free of defects, and yet they still go out of business.

---

[22]John Guspari, *I Know It When I See It* (New York: AMACOM, 1985).

They go out of business because of the process that they used to operationally define the Voice of the Customer. While they are happy that they make the best and most precisely blue products in the business, the bulk of the market wanted red products and did not particularly care what shade of red it was.

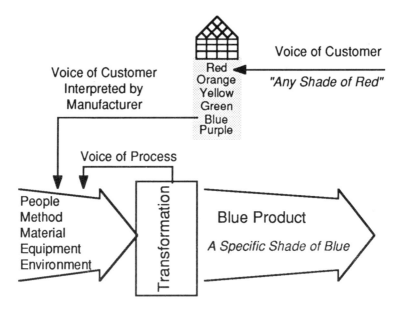

Figure 5.30
Listening to Only a Portion of the Market

Another gap is caused by some leaders who urge their people to think and act as if they owned the business. Their underlying logic is that the employees would make better decisions if they "thought like owners." They would be more careful with spending money—and in fact, in everything they did. The problem is that the leaders have not spent the time with the employees to operationally define how an owner should act. Each employee will operationalize the request as best he can, in his own different way (Figure 5.31). At General Motors, we call this process "aligning the arrows" (Figure 5.32). This is vitally important to GM, because our strength has been in our individual people and sometimes, they are not all aimed in the same direction.

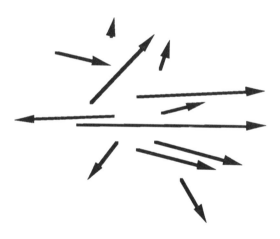

Figure 5.31
Everyone "Just Doing His Best"

The leadership must operationally define its Vision, and Mission, and Beliefs and Values so that the employees can more consistently accomplish them. This alignment is a prelude to the increase of teamwork and the eventual balance of individual and team.

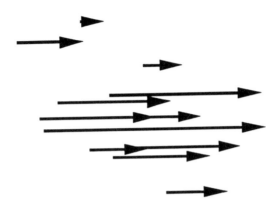

Figure 5.32
Aligning the Arrows

The operational definition of any command, policy, procedure, or request is not what you intended, but what the process actually gave you.

23

---

[23]Dik Browne, "Hagar the Horrible," Dik Browne.

Percy Bridgman coined the words *operational definition*, as he recognized;

> ... that the ultimately important thing about any theory is what it actually does, not what it says it does or what its author thinks it does, for these are often very different things indeed...[24]

C.I. Lewis wrote about Pure Concepts as

> ... that meaning which must be common to two minds when they understand each other by the use of a substantive or its equivalent.[25]

Walter Shewhart and W. Edwards Deming have continued to operationalize Bridgman's work. According to Dr. Deming:

> An operational definition is one that people can do business with. An operational definition of safe, round, reliable, or any other quality must be communicable, with the same meaning to vendor as to purchaser, same meaning yesterday and today to the production worker. Example:
>
> 1. A specific test of a piece of material or an assembly
>
> 2. A criterion (or criteria) for judgement

[24]P. W. Bridgman, *The Nature of Physical Theory* (Princeton: Princeton University Press, 1936).

[25]C.I. Lewis, *Mind and the World Order* (New York: Dover Publications, 1929).

3. Decision: (yes or no) the object or the
   material did or did not meet the
   criterion (or criteria).

What is the meaning of the law that butter for
sale must be 80 per cent butterfat? Does it mean
80 per cent butterfat, or more, in every pound that
you buy? Or does it mean 80 per cent on the average? What would you mean by 80 per cent butterfat on the average? The average over your purchases of butter during a year? Or would you
mean the average production of all butter for a
year, yours and other people's purchases of butter
from a particular source? How many pounds
would you test, for calculation of the average?
How would you select butter for test? Would you
be concerned with the variation in butterfat from
pound to pound? Obviously, any attempt to define
operationally 80 per cent butterfat runs headlong
into the need for statistical techniques and criteria. Again, the words 80 per cent butterfat, by
themselves have no meaning.[26]

Operational definitions link specific concepts to
percepts. Science and philosophy are not as exacting
as business. If you are stumped in science or philosophy, you can ponder it a bit or go on to a different problem to solve. If you are stumped in business, you must

---

[26]W. Edwards Deming, *Out of the Crisis* (Cambridge: MIT CAES,
1982).

do something today or you might be out of business tomorrow. Philosophers do not have to operationalize their concepts, but business people do.

"What I especially like about being a philosopher-scientist is that I don't have to get my hands dirty."

27

Operational definitions are the link between the letter of the law and the spirit of the law. No amount of unilateral specificity can convey the spirit or the intent of the law. That requires at least two-way understanding *and* an alignment of values. This is one of

---

[27]Sidney Harris (used with his permission).

the reasons why Dr. Deming believes that knowledge of some theory of psychology is important.

Theory of Psychology

- Knowledge of psychology helps us to understand people, interactions between people, the dynamics of groups, the interactions between groups and individuals, and any system of management.

- People are different from one another. A leader must be aware of these differences and use them for optimization of everybody's abilities and inclinations.

- People learn in different ways, and at different speeds.

- A leader has an obligation to improve systems.

- There is intrinsic motivation, extrinsic motivation, and over-justification.

In Chapter 3, I defined psychology as the intersection of emotional and logical levels. The word is taken from the Greek "psyche," meaning soul, and "logos," meaning logic. This discussion on theory will be brief because its operationalization is the subject of Chapter 6. Remember as you read this, that Dr. Deming has said that one need not be an expert in all of the aspects of profound knowledge. I am not a psycholo-

gist—but then that seldom stops anybody from giving
advice! I do however, defer to my friends Dr. Edward
Baker, Dr. Wendy Coles, Dr. Robert Klekamp, and Mr.
Peter Scholtes, when it comes to psychology. I have
learned much from them and others.

> ...the prosperity of countries depends on their abil-
> ity to create value through their people, and not
> by husbanding resources and technologies.[28]

People are our most important resource. This is
easy to say, but hard to understand, and even harder
to operationalize. The difficulty arises because people
are different from each other, and from all other resources. The methods that produce prosperity in the
mechanical world may cause bare subsistence in the
living world. My guiding principle, as I work with people, is the belief that they first need to feel important
as individuals, and then they also need to feel like an
important part of a family, or society, or team. The
balance between these needs is vital.

My view of psychology is a balance of its three
main theories: behavioral (physical), cognitive (logical), and psychodynamic (emotional). I believe that
each school of thought contributes a valuable perspective, but no single view is complete in itself. The na-
ture-versus-nurture discussion in the theory of psychology is similar to the *a priori*-versus-empirical discussion in the theory of knowledge.

---

[28]Kenichi Ohmae, *The Borderless World* ©1990 by McKinsey &
    Co., Inc. Used by permission of Harper Business, a division of
    HarperCollins of New York.

From my perspective as a statistician, I see that the performance of the process is a function of the within-subgroup variability and the between-subgroup variability. In human terms, this means that we must optimize the variability within the person, and the variability between the person and other people and the other process resources. You cannot optimize one without affecting the other. This optimization must balance the need to reduce variability with the need to increase the number of perspectives.

We need to go beyond "tricks" or manipulation. Many people recognize when they are being manipulated, and they don't appreciate it. Peter Scholtes tells about a time during which he was answering an irate boss with his best active listening techniques. His boss would say something and Peter would mirror, "Sounds like you feel really disappointed"—to which his boss finally replied, "Don't use that workshop stuff on me" —or words to that effect. You can apply tools to machines, for their improvement, and they won't become defensive. But the insensitive use of "psychological" tools on people may quickly become a different story.

The tools, or tricks, that I am talking about take advantage of people's need to feel good about themselves. "Foot-in-the-door" and "door-in-the-face" are two well known examples. To get a person to do something, you might get your foot in the door by asking him to do a "little something" that makes him feel good about himself. You will then have an advantage in getting him to do something much larger or harder. Another trick is to ask for something so large that he slams the door in your face, and later agrees to something less because he feels badly about his behavior. This is manipulative, not motivational, and the person who really understands psychology, and cares about people, will avoid using such tricks.

> Psychologists consider three ways to achieve one's goals: competitively, which means working against others; cooperatively, which means working with others; and independently, which means working without regard to others.[29]

This view fits with my world view of dependent, independent, and interdependent actions as illustrated in Figure 5.33.

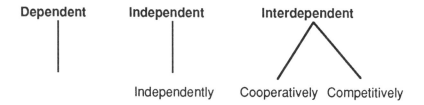

Dependent   **Independent**   **Interdependent**

Independently   Cooperatively   Competitively

Figure 5.33
Three Ways to Achieve One's Goals

I think that Kohn misses one important way that some people use to achieve their goals—dependency—to allow oneself to be swept along, like driftwood in a tide. People need to grow out of the depen-

---

[29]Alfie Kohn, *The Case Against Competition* (Boston: Houghton Mifflin Co.,1986).

dent mode as they mature, but dependency is still a way that numerous people operate. My view of cooperation and competition differs slightly from Kohn, as I see them as forms of interdependency, which, of course, needs to be balanced with independence. Given that balance, you can choose to compete or cooperate. Optimization almost always requires cooperation. Competition is usually a zero-sum game. Its aim is to take the market share away from someone else. Cooperation is usually not a zero-sum game because its aim is to increase the total market.

People are different. But as Dr. Deming said to a Deming Users Group in San Diego, "Yes we are all different from one another, but in the important things we are all alike." And we are all alike in our need to feel important as individuals and as part of a group. A leader must recognize these similarities, in addition to the differences, using both to optimize the process. Figure 5.34 summarizes my method of achieving this.

In the **Physical** and **Individual** cells, I find that a short personal note can help make the recipient feel important. The note can be a thank-you, or what I prefer, a note of confidence in the ability of the person. Dr. Deming takes time to answer all of his letters, making each of his correspondents feel very important. Dr. Deming also has a way with words that makes one feel important. He frequently says of a colleague, "There is no one better!" It makes you feel great to know that he means you are a part of the process. There is no one better and there is no one worse.

	Individual	Family
Physical	• Send personal note of confidence or appreciation • Take time to listen to the person • Provide opportunities to hone skills • Encourage personal fitness, health, safety • Give someone responsibility for a process • Acknowledge person's presence	• Include in official organization • Take time to listen to groups • Establish common eating areas • Provide team uniform • Emphasize that all skills are vital • No-fault help for members of team
Logical	• Promote with emphasis on transformation • Ask someone to teach others • Highlight brilliant contributions to knowledge • Ask someone to represent the group	• Promote from within and on seniority • Educate team together • Emphasize suggestions of the team • Encourage participation in social memory • Share knowledge with others
Emotional	• Invest with congruent resources • Highlight the values you wish to operationalize • Laugh • Build on legacy and immortality • Commend someone for knowledge and care	• Emphasize belonging to team no matter what • Cry together • Highlight sense of stewardship and cause

Figure 5.34
Physical, Logical, and Emotional Ways
To Help An Individual Feel Important
And Part of A Family

I find it helpful to simply acknowledge someone's presence.

I find it helpful to listen to a person in order to make that individual feel important. It is one of the key attributes of a leader, discussed in Chapter 4. Time is a very precious commodity and people appreciate the time you invest in listening to their message. I try to focus on the present when I listen, trying not to think ahead to my response or other subjects, because that takes away my ability to listen well.[30]

I find it helpful to invest in the development of skills for a person. The investment in training tells that person that you think he or she is important, not only today, but to the future of the organization.

I find it helpful to invest in fitness, health, and safety, in order to make a person feel important.

I find it helpful to give responsibility, or ownership of a process, to help make a person feel important.

I find it helpful to write quotes from people as they speak. It sends the signal that I think they have said something very important.

In the **Physical** and **Family** cells, people need to be included in the official organization. The process by which they are included should not deprive others from also feeling important as individuals. For exam-

---

[30]A good discussion of listening is found in A.H. Maslow's *The Farther Reaches of Human Nature* (New York: Penguin Books, 1971).

ple, think back on how you felt when you were the last person selected for a team in whatever "friendly" games children play.

I find it helpful to listen to teams or small groups of people. This strengthens the bonds between them. Sometimes these meetings will serve as a catharsis and so must be managed with great care, in order to end with a positive bond.

I find it helpful to establish common eating, meeting, or work areas. This helps reinforce the bonds of a team. Likewise, uniforms, ball caps, or other apparel are physical evidence of team membership.

I find it helpful to emphasize the importance of all skills to the prosperity of a team. This strengthens the bonds of the team.

I find it helpful to have a policy of no-fault help for members of the team. This encourages communication and strengthens the bonds of the team.

In the **Logical** and **Individual** cells, I find it helpful to promote someone for his potential ability to lead in transformation. This sends a signal to others that the leadership considers this to be worthwhile.

I find it helpful to ask someone with knowledge to teach others.

I find it helpful to highlight someone's good contribution to knowledge.

I find it helpful to ask an individual to represent the group in a meaningful way.

In the **Logical** and **Family** cells, I find it helpful to promote from within the organization.

I find it helpful to educate and train the team together.

I find it helpful to emphasize suggestions for improvement which come from the team.

I find it helpful to emphasize group participation in the development of social memory.

I find it helpful to share information with others, again, as a team.

In the **Emotional** and **Individual** cell, I find it important to invest, in a particular person, those extrinsic resources which are congruent with specific intrinsic motivators.

I find it helpful to highlight values that you hope the team will operationalize.

I find it helpful to appreciate a person's sense of humor. You need to laugh with people. This is a strong bonding activity.

I find it helpful to build on the universal concern for mortality. I emphasize the legacy each can leave.

In the **Emotional** and **Family** cell, I find it helpful to emphasize our lifetime commitment to each other. No matter what you do, you will be a member of the group or family.

I find it helpful to be able to cry, or mourn appropriately, with the group or family.

I find it helpful to emphasize responsibilities of stewardship and working for a cause. There is a song in Cameron Mackintosh's production of *Les Miserables* that is particularly appropriate here:[31]

> When the beating of your heart echoes the beating of the drums, there is a life about to start when tomorrow comes!

Dr. Deming highlights the fact that people learn in different ways. I have difficulty remembering that just because I have some percept, concept, or emotive, that everyone might not be affected in the same way. I should know better—I learned long ago that what is obvious to me, isn't necessarily obvious to others, and vice versa.

Statistical thinking is critical to personal improvement. There are few things that create more frustration and anxiety than a series of apparently random rewards or punishments for one's actions. And this will usually be the case with processes that operate similarly to the red bead experiment. People are rewarded one day for producing only 5 red beads and castigated the next for producing 15. The person was trying his best and the process was the same on both days. Who wouldn't be frustrated under these conditions? This need for statistical thinking is paramount in my thoughts as I work with individuals and groups.

---

[31]"Do You Hear the People Sing" from the musicale "LES MISERABLES" by Alain Boublil and Claude-Michel Schöberg. Published by Alain Boublil Music Ltd.

Education and Training

"A man who reviews the old so as to learn the new,
is qualified to teach others." (Confucius)[32]

Why do we study the history of any science?
Current work, so one would think, will preserve
whatever is still useful of the work of preceding
generations... Teachers or students who attempt
to act upon the theory that the most recent treatise is all they need will soon discover that they
are making things unnecessarily difficult for
themselves ... any treatise that attempts to render
the present state of science really renders methods, problems, and results that are historically
conditioned and are meaningful only with refer-
ence to the historical background from which they
spring. To put the same thing somewhat differently: the state of any science at any given time
implies its past history and cannot be satisfacto-
rily conveyed without making this implicit history
explicit... We learn to understand why we are as
far as we actually are and also why we are not
further. [33]

I think that Schumpeter's statement is critical
to the success of any attempt for change, and especially any attempt to educate and train. Unlike elec-

---

[32]Confucius, *The Analects of Confucius*, trans. Arthur Whaley
(London: HarperCollins, 1948).

[33]Joseph A. Schumpeter, *History of Economic Analysis* (New
York: Oxford University Press, 1954).

tronics or medicine where the new completely outpaces the old, many "old" methods of teaching are very useful today.

> Richard Mulcaster in the year 1611 argued that teachers should respect the differences between individual children, that not age but readiness should determine the curriculum for each pupil, and that the ablest teachers should be assigned to the earliest grades.[34]

Sound familiar? How about some older advice? Plato, in his Republic said:

> The elements of instruction...should be presented to the mind in childhood, but not with any compulsion;...Knowledge which is acquired under compulsion has no hold on the mind. Therefore do not use compulsion, but let early education be rather a sort of amusement; this will better enable you to find out the natural bent of the child.[35]

One form of compulsion in Western cultures is the emphasis on individual performance. Carried to its extreme, it results in an emphasis in competition between people that reduces the excellence for all participants. It starts early.

---

[34]Daniel Boorstin, *The Discoverers: A History of Man's Search to Know His World and Himself* (New York: Vintage Books Division of Random House, 1985).

[35]Will Durant, *The Story of Philosophy* (New York: Simon & Schuster, 1953).

As youngsters move from home or preschool into
the larger, more competitive world of elementary
school, they begin to make judgments about their
own abilities. If they feel inadequate, they may
give up.[36]

If they give up, they will drop out. If they drop
out, they will look for ways to feel important on their
own terms. And when they do that, we all suffer. Our
society, just doing its best (without the aid of adequate
statistical thinking), has carefully taught us that to be
below average is cause for shame. *No one should be
below average. No one should be a loser.* This theory
should be discarded, but there are many people who
have no other perspective. Even educators do not
know this—how could they in today's atmosphere of
testing and evaluation, aimed at the ranking of students and teachers.

If people know how to think statistically, you
would not continue to find headlines and articles like:

Half of state residents give schools above-average grades.[37]

Teachers' pay climbs past $25,000 mark. 31 states are below the national average.[38]

---

[36]Barbara Kantrowitz and Pat Wingert, "How Kids Learn," (April
17, 1989, © 1989 by *Newsweek*, Used by permission).
[37]*The Saginaw NEWS*, September 11,1990.
[38]*USA Today*, April 24, 1986.

In nearly any collection of measurements, about half will be above and below the arithmetical average. This is a known fact before any data is collected. If the measurements came from a stable process, then the same process that produced the below-average numbers, also produced those which were above average.

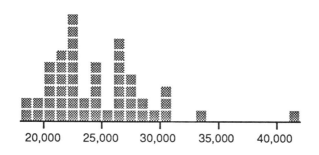

Figure 5.35
Average Teacher's Salaries by State [39]

The only outcome in Figure 5.35 that looks special to me is the one state that paid an average salary of $41,000. But I know, before any data is collected, that about half will be below average. People without statistical knowledge, who are below average feel they must change in order to be above average. They com-

---

[39]*USA Today*, April 24, 1986.

pete with others for those limited positions in the up-
per range, or try to collectively raise their group
salary. But as they improve their salaries, the average
also improves and so there are still about half below
the new average.

The late education critic, John Holt, made clear
the price we pay for competition in the classroom:

> We destroy the ... love of learning in children,
> which is so strong when they are small, by en-
> couraging and compelling them to work for petty
> and contemptible rewards—gold stars, or papers
> marked 100 and tacked to the wall, or A's on re-
> port cards, or honor rolls, or dean's lists, or Phi
> Beta Kappa keys—in short, for the ignoble satis-
> faction of feeling that they are better than some-
> one else.[40]

Holt is criticizing classrooms in the United States. Dr.
Deming criticizes them too, but he is trying to move
the pendulum, now locked squarely on rugged individualism and competition, to a more balanced view between individual importance and team importance.

Dr. Deming does not use compulsion—even in
graduate courses. He has a way of making every student feel important individually, as well as important
parts of a "family." When he was my teacher at NYU,
he listened to our contributions in class and wrote
careful comment on our papers. I thought that his ex-

---

[40]Alfie Kohn, *The Case Against Competition* (Boston: Houghton-
Miflin Co., 1986).

position of the subject matter was fun. It was a balance of theory and application, told by a master storyteller, to people who wished to learn. One story that he doesn't tell much anymore (because it could appear self-serving), concerns an important concept he indirectly learned from R. A. Fisher. It goes something like this:

> If you had to give Fisher a grade as a teacher, it would have to be a zero because there is not a lower grade. The classroom was cold and damp, he would come into the room with the ink not yet dry on his notes, he would make mistakes at the blackboard that the students would correct; in fact you had to sit in the front row to make out the illegible handwriting. Why then, did people from around the world come and crowd his classrooms? Because they wanted to see and hear what a great mind was thinking about. What questions did he ask and what problems did he consider important?[41]

I think this is one of the reasons why Dr. Deming's seminars are filled to capacity. There are still many people who want to see and hear that which a great mind is thinking.

Remember, you cannot ask questions without theory. And one of the best sources for theory should be education. But, as Bertrand Russell observed:

---

[41]Conversation with Dr. Deming about R.A. Fisher.

> Education has two very different purposes: on the
> one hand it aims at developing the individual and
> giving him knowledge which will be useful to him;
> on the other hand it aims at producing citizens
> who will be convenient for the State or Church
> which is educating them.[42]

Daniel Boorstin uses different words, but comes to the same conclusion.

> Europe's ancient institutions of learning, colleges
> and universities, had been founded not to discover
> the new but to transmit a heritage.[43]

It seems that today's schools of business could learn a lesson here. Right now they mostly perpetuate the status quo, while entrepreneurial people in business are the ones who develop the new theories. Faculties of business schools are relegated to be nothing more than modern day troubadours, spreading the gossip of what has happened in one or another company or country. It is easy to explain past events. And while knowledge is required to explain the past, the temporal spread goes at least two ways. The job of a leader is to predict. He is interested in the future. I see the job of educators to balance the past and the future.

---

[42]Bertrand Russell, *The Scientific Outlook* (New York: W.W. Norton and Company, 1931).

[43]Daniel Boorstin, *The Discoverers: A History of Man's Search to Know His World and Himself* (New York: Vintage Books Division of Random House, 1985).

The gap, however, continues to be enormous. Even before President Bush announced his vision of being known as the "education president," corporations in the US were spending $25 billion a year just for remedial literacy programs[44] because their employees were not prepared to meet the demands needed in today's new economic age. More recent figures, which include the remediation built into the education process, put the cost at around $100 billion a year.[45] Industry cannot continue to "rework" its employees any more than it can afford to rework its products. We must work upstream with our suppliers of educated and trained business people.

What can we do? Our approach should be the same as our approach to the improvement of any process: follow the 8 Steps in the PDSA cycle. There needs to be physical change, logical change, and emotional change. Schools and companies everywhere should begin teaching their students how to improve processes. This facet of intellectual capital is just as vital as the knowledge of any other specific science in today's new economic age.

> In the high-value businesses, profits derive not from scale and volume but from an ongoing discovery of connections between the solutions to problems and the identification of new needs.[46]

Only people with knowledge can fill this need.

---

[44]Stephen Garrison, *Fortune Magazine,* March 26,1990.
[45]James Dezell, *IBM Directions*, White Plains, Winter 1990-1991.
[46]Robert Reich, "The Real Economy," *The Atlantic Monthly*, February 1991.

Tools	\multicolumn{8}{c}{Steps in PDSA Cycle}							
	1	2	3	4	5	6	7	8
Box and Whisker Plots						●		
Brainstorming			●	●			●	
Cause and Effect Diagrams		●		●			●	
Check Sheets				●				
Control Charts	●						●	
Creative Problem Solving				●			●	
Design of Experiments					●			
Failure Mode Analysis			●					
Failure Mode and Effects Analysis			●					
Fault Tree Analysis			●					
Force Field Analysis			●					
Gantt / Pie Charts				●				
Histograms and Run Charts	●					●		
Impact Matrices				●			●	
Listening	●	●		●		●	●	●
Loss Function	●					●		●
Operational Definitions	●			●		●		●
Pareto Diagrams				●				●
Process Flow Charts		●	●				●	
Quality Function Deployment	●			●		●		●
Regression Analysis	●			●	●	●		
Reliability Analysis					●			
Scatter Diagrams	●			●		●		
Simulation					●			
Surveys	●	●				●	●	
Systems Analysis				●	●			
Teambuilding				●			●	
Time Series Forecasting	●					●		
Visioning			●				●	

Figure 5.36
Socio-Technical Methods for Improvement

At the very least, teams of students should be able to use the socio-technical tools that are a part of the PDSA cycle. By this I mean that they need knowledge, not just an awareness of the buzz-words. Each tool has a specific use—no tool is universal. There also is no "instant pudding." A few years ago I would be asked in seminars and meetings, "Where can I use a control chart?" After that, it was, "Where can I do a Taguchi experiment?" Then, it became, "Where can I do Quality Function Deployment?" Now it is, "Where can I do simultaneous engineering?" And it is anyone's guess what tomorrow's students will think the miracle tool to be. Everyone is looking for that "silver bullet" that will quickly strike right at the heart of the problem. To paraphrase an old saying, if the only tool you have is a hammer, its surprising how many things start to look like a nail.

It is not my purpose in this book to educate you in socio-technical methods, although a listing of them is located in Figure 5.36. I will however, refer you to a number of books and videos that I think are particularly useful:

Brassard, **The Memory Jogger Plus**, GOAL/QPC, Methuen, 1989.

Chambers & Wheeler, **Understanding Statistical Process Control**, SPC Press, Inc., Knoxville, 1986.

Ishikawa, **Guide To Quality Control**, Asian Productivity Organization, Tokyo, 1976.

Jessup, **Continuing Process Control and Process Capability Improvement**, Ford Motor Company, Dearborn, various.

Kane, **Defect Prevention**, Marcel Dekker, New York, 1989.

King, **Better Designs in Half the Time**, GOAL/QPC, Methuen, 1987.

Latzko, **Quality and Productivity for Bankers and Financial Managers**, Marcel Dekker, New York, 1986.

Scholtes, **The Team Handbook**, Joiner Associates, Madison, 1988.

Schwinn, **Transformation of American Industry Training System**, PQ Systems Inc., Dayton, 1984.

Tribus, **Deployment Flow Charting**, videotape and manual. Quality & Productivity, Inc., Los Angeles, 1989.

Wheeler, **Understanding Industrial Experimentation,** 2nd Ed., SPC Press, Knoxville, 1990.

Dimensional Control Plan - Videotape by Ford Motor Company.

Statistical Methods and FTQE, Videotape by Ford Motor Company.

Quadratic Loss Function - Videotape by Ford Motor Company.

This list is not meant to be all inclusive and my previous statement, that I do not agree with the entire contents of any book or video, needs to be repeated. In Chapter 6, I will show how these methods are used as a help to leaders in their jobs.

Grading and Evaluation

Many people do not understand Dr. Deming's position on grades in school or his position on ratings in the workplace. I will specifically discuss the appraisal of people in Chapter 6, but the theory is the same. Dr. Deming says that students should not be denied meaningful feedback pertaining to their progress. Students are, after all, involved in a process of learning, and every process has a Voice of the Customer and a Voice of the Process. For example, a student wishes to gain some knowledge about accounting. He seeks a teacher who may prescribe a course of study in accounting. This is Plan. Together they carry out the plan of study. This is Do. As they operationalize the Plan, they must study what they learned. This is Study. They may or may not adjust their resources depending on what they learned. This is Act. Then they proceed to Plan again. Each stage requires them to listen to the Voice of the Process and take action that is appropriate to match the Voice of the Customer.

A leader's job is prediction. Do grades aid in prediction? Not in themselves. A student might develop some knowledge of the world from the perspectives that are presented in his course of study. It may be conceptual or empirical knowledge. By definition, his percepts, concepts, and emotives are stable over time. His grades may be stable over time as well. In fact, for prediction, they must be. But the key to the usefulness of the prediction is the link of the perspectives gained in the course of study to the perspectives needed in the application of the knowledge in his job.

This is similar to a situation where a process must proceed from a prototype stage to a full production stage. It may be stable in the prototype stage, but if the production stage is a different process, stability may be a minor factor in your ability to predict performance in the production stage. You might get straight A's in school as you learn about confidence intervals, ANOVA, and hypothesis testing, but that may have little bearing on anyone's prediction of your usefulness in industry.

If there are grades, then the aim should be to improve both teacher and student. Profound knowledge can be used to construct a process that accomplishes this aim. From the perspective of the student, she wishes to improve her knowledge of the subject matter. From the perspective of the teacher, he wishes to improve the knowledge of all of the students and to get better at it.

Frank Murdock of Ford first used this method of grades to help him improve his teaching. I think it is a good use of grades. Dr. David Henderson of General Motors provided these data for a course that he taught at Washington University. The process is outlined for you.

People:	Teacher and at least 10 students.
Material:	100 questions that cover the scope of the entire course.
Equipment:	Random number tables.
Environment:	Encouragement to learn, free from fear.

Method: Use random numbers to select the ten questions to be
answered in each weekly
test. Each week there is an
equal probability that any of
the 100 questions could be
asked.

A chart that protects the identity of each individual is updated every week. The completed chart
can be interpreted as follows in Figure 5.37.

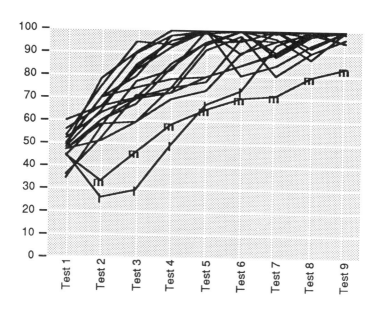

Figure 5.37
A Method of Using Grades for Improvement

You can see that in **Test 1**, the scores averaged about 50, had a high of about 60, and a low of about 35. The actions that a teacher takes should be guided by listening to the Voice of the Process. Is the process stable? Now there is not enough data to make that determination, but he can take some comfort that the data are relatively close together with no apparent special outliers. He might be uncomfortable with scores so high for the first class. The course or the questions may not be challenging enough.

On **Test 2**, the scores improved. There were two students who might be in need of special attention. Their scores were apart from the rest.

On **Test 3**, the scores again improved. The two students whose scores were apart from the rest are still apart from the rest, but not as obviously. The teacher might notice an increase in the range of scores.

On **Test 4**, the scores continue to improve. The range of scores begins to decrease. The two students whose scores were apart from the rest continue to be low.

On **Tests 5** through **9**, you see the emergence of a pattern. Most of the class are tightly grouped in the high 90's. They are all part of the same process. The teacher should have a high degree of belief that they are able to consistently answer the questions that he asked. The scores of one student have consistently remained apart from the rest: he will need special help to improve. This pattern of test results could also signal to the teacher that he could have further challenged the students who began to "max out" by week 4.

One strength of this method is that it does not highlight those above or below average. This lessens the chance of unwarranted despair or elation. It helps focus the teacher and students to learn theory and to improve knowledge.

Theory leads to questions. These are the questions that I consider important:

- What will get your customers to take joy in your product or service?
- What value will you add to the answer of any question that you ask?
- What will you postpone or cancel to answer this question?
- What process will you use to come up with the answer?
- What are the tradeoffs?
- What will get your employees to take joy in their work?

You will notice that these questions begin and end with the concept of joy.

What will make customers take joy in your product or service? This question is from the theory that customers are not only influenced by the lack of negatives but also by the presence of positives. In the automotive business, there is little correlation between the positives and negatives on a world-class level. This means that the degree of satisfaction that a customer takes in his vehicle is usually independent of the number of problems that he has with the vehicle.

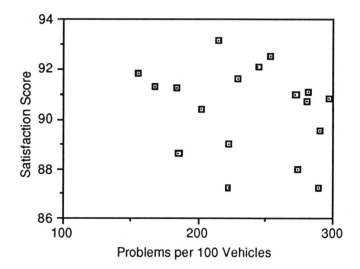

Figure 5.38
Satisfaction of Automobile Owners

Your plans to improve must include the increase in positives as well as the decrease of negatives. Unless you ask this question, you will not be able to increase the joy that your customers take in your product or service.

What value will you add to the answer of any question that you ask? The theory behind this question is the process model. The answer to your question is input to which you must add value and then pass it on to your customer. If you do not know what value you will add to the answer, you should not ask the question. Remember, the only reason to collect data is to take action. That action can be in the obvious physical sense, the logical sense as in knowledge, or the emotional sense.

What will you postpone or cancel in order to answer this question? The theory behind this question is that there is only 24 hours in a day and if you answer this question, you are not able to do something else. You should not have people standing around waiting for you to ask a question. If there are high levels of fear in your organization, you might do better not to require an immediate answer. You should, however, ask that everyone keep a tally of what is postponed or rescheduled or cancelled. After about a month, you may see a pattern of items that are consistently pushed off the plate. You may then officially and intelligently take them off the plate. This is a vital step in the removal of barriers to improvement.

What process will you use to come up with the answer? This question is rooted in the theory of knowledge. Questions are cheap; it's the answers that cost money, and some answers cost a lot more than others. You must know *how* an answer is generated in order to add value to it. You must know its strengths and its weaknesses. This is no different than any other process, such as the "clean the table" story in Chapter 4. I cannot clean this table unless you tell me for what purpose you will use it. If the question-asker does not ask you to describe the process that you will use to formulate the answer, you must take the initiative and tell him "how you will clean the table."

I was once asked by a vice president, "What is the labor content in a particular purchased commodity?"

I did my part. "What are you going to use the table for?—What are you going to do with the answer?"

He said it was to justify a bonus, dependent upon the reduction labor content in the commodity. So I told him it would be 15%. At first he was impressed, but after a few moments he asked, "How did you come up with 15%?" I told him that was the most intelligent question that he had asked. I could have written the question on my notepad and sent him a memo the next week, with the answer of 15%, and he would have used the number without hesitation. But he would have had no idea what process I used to generate that number. I see time and time again where data are used for strategic decisions—and there is no knowledge about the process used to generate the data.

What are the tradeoffs? The theory behind this question is that many processes are interdependent. If you change one, others are affected. You must aim to optimize the process. In order to quickly cut costs, you may call for the elimination of overtime. But you know before you cut the overtime, that you will soon be asking what happened to the schedule. You have probably solved nearly every industrial problem several times during your career. And in so doing, you have probably created many other problems.

Water leaks are one such problem for all auto makers—whether German, Japanese, or American. All automobile companies have dedicated teams of people to solve water-leak problems in vehicles. All auto makers have successfully solved water leak problems, but in doing so, have created door-closing problems. But that is another team's problem, which they probably solve with relish. Unfortunately their solution only makes necessary yet another team.

List of : __Door Closing Problems__   Criteria for Synergy:

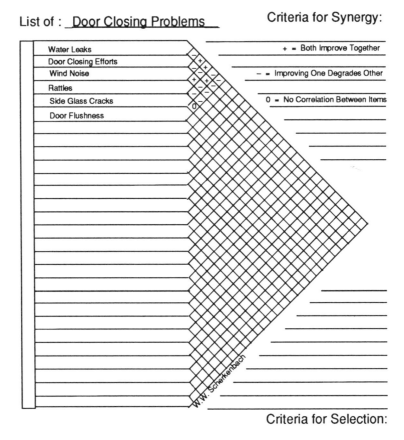

+ = Both Improve Together

– = Improving One Degrades Other

0 = No Correlation Between Items

Water Leaks
Door Closing Efforts
Wind Noise
Rattles
Side Glass Cracks
Door Flushness

Criteria for Selection:

Figure 5.39
The Problem of Trade-offs

You can stop this vicious cycle and turn it into a virtuous one by making a list of all of the effects of solving water leak problems (See Figure 5.39). Certainly there has been the negative effect of doors that are harder to close. There has been the positive effect of a reduction in wind noise. If water doesn't leak in, air might not either. If you must slam the door to get it to close, however, you might experience side glass breakage. If your solution involved the weatherstrip, door flushness and door margins might be affected. The list is longer than this and can usually be assembled in a few hours of brain-storming. This activity is a vital part of steps 4 and 7 in the Continual Improvement cycle.

What will get your employees to take joy in their work? The theory behind this question is the subject of Chapter 6. There is no substitute for spending time with your people so that you know them. In time, you will know what promotes joy in their work, and how you may help them.

But first you must understand the theory behind the loss function. It is this perspective of the Voice of the Customer, that breaks the paradigm that the elimination of defects is all you must have to prosper.

My view of the loss function is that it is purely from the Voice of the Customer. Others see it as the sum of the loss to the producer and the consumer.

I mentioned in Chapter 1 that one way to dimension the Voice of the Customer is through "goalposts" or specification limits (see Figure 5.40).

These "goalposts" can be used to estimate the loss to the customer when a product or service varies in a particular measure. The "goalpost" model says that there is no loss to the customer when the product or service stays anywhere within the "goalposts." If the product or service strays anywhere outside of the goalposts, then the customer incurs the full brunt of the loss. This model is useful in isolated situations. For instance, you incur no loss if you are on the train when it leaves the station, but you incur total loss if you are not on the train. Even these situations have limitations: you would incur a gradually-increasing loss if you arrived at the train station two days before your train was scheduled to depart.

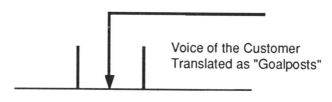

Figure 5.40
Voice of the Customer as "Goal Posts"

Since I do not use equations in this coverage of loss function, to learn about the more technical aspects of loss function, I recommend any of the following:

Thomas Barker, **"Quality Engineering by Design - The Taguchi Approach,"** *AQC Transactions*, 1985.

Peter T. Jessup, **"Process Capability, The Value of Improved Performance,"** paper presented at the ASQC Automotive Division Workshop Seminar, November 1983.

Kailash C. Kapur, **"Quality Loss Function and Inspection,"** *Proceedings Test, Measurement and Inspection for Quality Control*, September 1987.

Victor Kane, **"Process Capability Indices,"** *Journal of Quality Technology, vol.18*, 1986.

Jerry Roslund, "**Evaluating Management Objectives With the Quality Loss Function**," *Quality Progress*, August 1989.

William Scherkenbach, *The Deming Route to Quality and Productivity: Road Maps and Roadblocks*, CEEPress, 1986.

Genichi Taguchi, *Introduction to Quality Engineering*, Asian Productivity Organization, 1986.

Donald Wheeler, *Understanding Industrial Experimentation*, 2nd Ed., SPC Press, Inc., 1990.

Every process manager must determine what customers desire and what the process actually delivers. This is the first step in the improvement of the process. You must determine the Gap. Loss functions should not be foreign to you. You probably use them implicitly in the every day conduct of your business. Mechanical engineers use stress strain curves. The cumulative stress curve is a loss function.

Pete Jessup originally constructed the following temperature example to demystify the notion of a quadratic loss function. Let's say that you are a customer at a seminar on leadership. There are People, Material, Method, Equipment, and Environment that comprise the process. One characteristic of the environment that affects your learning is the temperature of the room in which you sit. Other characteristics that affect your learning might be the acoustics, the seating, and the lighting. As you feel warmer and warmer, you might take your jacket off and think about how warm it is getting. You may even fall asleep. As you feel cooler and cooler, you might begin to shiver, put your jacket back on, and leave your seat to walk around. You may even leave the room. In either case, you loose some information that is supposed to be transferred to you. At what temperature should you set the room?

Ask 20 people in the audience, "At what temperature would you say that the room is beginning to get warmer than you really like?" One audience provided the answers charted in Figure 5.41.

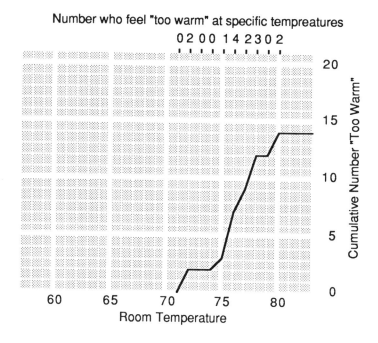

Figure 5.41
Losses Due to Warmer Room Temperatures

Different people have different thresholds for warmth. There is no one temperature where everyone is comfortable and at the next higher temperature, everyone is warmer than they really would like. Certainly, if the temperature is above 80 degrees, all of these people would be warmer than they really would like. At above 80 degrees there would be maximum loss due to warmth.

How about cold? Ask them, "At what temperature would you say that the room was beginning to get a bit cooler than you really like?" The same audience provided the answers in Figure 5.42

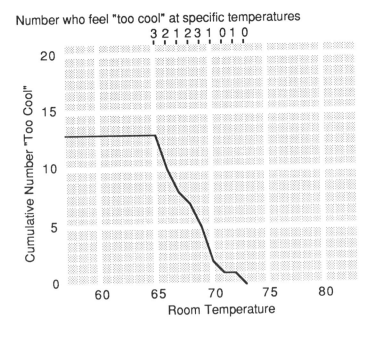

Figure 5.42
Losses Due to Cooler Room Temperatures

Different people have different thresholds for being cool. There is no one temperature where everyone is comfortable and at the next lower temperature everyone is cooler than they really would like. Certainly if the temperature is below 65 degree, all of these people would be cooler than they really would like. At below 65 degrees there would be maximum loss due to the coolness of the audience.

So at what temperature should we set the room? We must put the 2 temperature profiles together to answer that question. When we put them together, we get a loss function that looks more like a parabola than a goalpost see Figure 5.43).

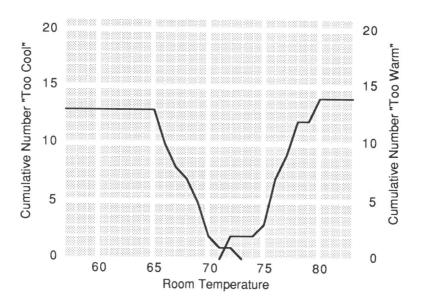

Figure 5.43
Loss Function for One Group of Customers

Is there any temperature of the room that would make everyone comfortable—that is, the room would be neither too warm nor too cool? No, because the warm and the cool profiles overlap. At what temperature of the room would there be the least loss to learning? Seventy-one degrees.

A more fundamental question should be asked about design. What size HVAC system is needed? To answer this question, we need to also listen to the Voice of the Process. In Figure 5.44, we see that an HVAC system that costs $20,000 may have a temperature profile that looks like curve A, while an HVAC system that costs $100,000 has a temperature profile that looks like curve B. Which should you install?

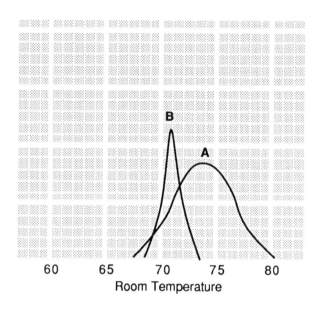

Figure 5.44
Voices of Two HVAC Processes

You need to compare the total cost to the producer and the cost to the customers. While the cost of HVAC system A is low, the loss to the customers is high. The loss for using system A with these customers is proportional to the shaded area in Figure 5.45.

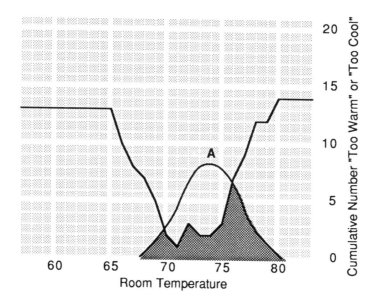

Figure 5.45
Loss Incurred with Process A

But the loss to the customers for using system B is proportional to the shaded area of Figure 5.46.

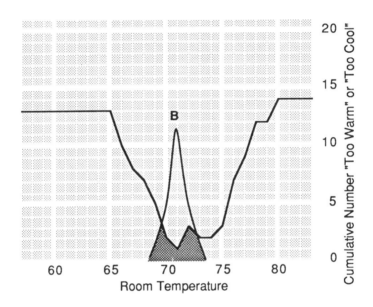

Figure 5.46
Loss Incurred with Process B

Even though the cost of system A is cheaper than system B, the total cost to customers and producer is less if system B is used.

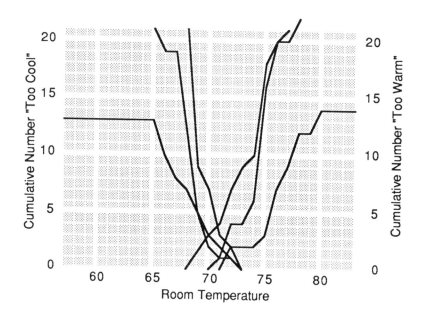

Figure 5.47
Loss Functions for Several Groups

We just evaluated a proposed product (temperature of a room) based on a survey of one group of customers. This is a fairly dangerous strategy. The pencil-thin line that bounds the Voice of the Customer is not as precise as it looks. And it only applies to the people you asked. You should listen to numbers of customers and at different times and locations to increase the number of perspectives that you have. In Figure 5.47 are the boundaries of three different groups of customers who attended my seminar. The three locations of the seminar were Newport Beach, Detroit, and

Rochester. You can begin to see the variability of the boundaries established by the three different groups of customers.

If the minimum loss is high, then you might consider segmenting the market into various niches. The loss from the customer's perspective depends on the shape of the loss function as well as its minimum. Most of the readings on the loss function stress the shape factor of the parabola. Some are low and indicate that the customers do not incur rapidly increasing loss over a given range. Some are high and indicate that the customers do incur rapidly increasing loss over a given range. I gave you a preview of these thoughts in Chapter 2 when I considered the losses to learning due to the acoustics and the seating and the lighting in addition to the temperature.

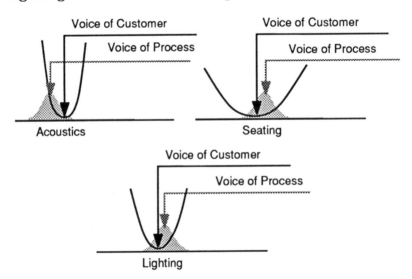

Figure 5.48
Loss Functions for Meeting Room

All of the loss functions were drawn with their minimums the same. This is an oversimplification that will hardly ever occur. If the loss functions for acoustics and seating look like this, then the choice of acoustics as being the obvious focus needs to be revised.

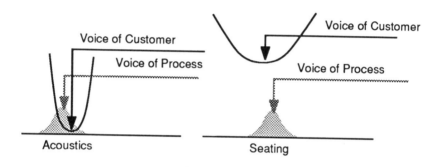

Figure 5.49
Selecting Critical Characteristics

The minimum loss should be very much a consideration when selecting critical characteristics.

The concept of the loss function is crucial to continual improvement. When you try to dimension your customers, keep this quadratic model and not the goalpost model in your mind. It is this piece of logic that begins to build the bridge from the letter of the law (physical) to the spirit of the law (emotional).

Chapter 6

Emotional Change

It is the *spirit* of the law that opens the possibility for us to reduce cost as we improve quality. It is the *spirit* of the law that opens the possibility for us to speak with one voice. It is the *spirit* of the law that opens the possibility for us to act with consistency of purpose.

> Schopenhauer said that nothing is more provoking, when we are arguing against a man with reasons and explanations, and taking all pains to convince him, than to discover at last that he will not understand, that we have to do with his will. Hence the uselessness of logic: no one ever convinced anybody by logic; and even logicians use logic only as a source of income. To convince a man, you must appeal to his self-interest, his desires, his will.[1]

Rousseau was right: above the logic of the head is the feeling in the heart. Pascal was right: the heart has reasons of its own, which the head can never un-

---

[1]Will Durant, *The Story of Philosophy* (New York: Washington Square Press, 1953).

derstand.[2] Dr. Deming observes that it is easier in the United Kingdom to "take Courage" than it is anywhere else—many public houses dispense it on demand. Difficult or not for the rest of us, we all need to take heart in business. Mencius said that it is the great man who does not lose his (originally good) child's heart.[3] Dr. Deming says that in western cultures, it is very, very difficult to become great because of what he calls forces of destruction.

> One is born with intrinsic motivation, self-esteem, dignity, curiosity, joy in learning. These attributes are high at the beginning of life, but are gradually crushed by the forces of destruction.[4]

He enumerates these forces as grades in school, merit system, incentive pay, targets, quotas, and suboptimization. I will elaborate on these later in this chapter. But first let's look at our aim. The absence of the forces of destruction will not foster joy in life. There need to be processes in place which foster strong positives, as the strong negatives are removed.

The aim is simple; I have mentioned it before. It is joy of ownership through joy of workmanship. Joy is an emotion. But there are other emotions and values that are also part of emotional change. A partial list (in no particular order) includes all of the following:

---

[2]Will Durant, *The Story of Philosophy* (New York: Washington Square Press, 1953).
[3]Wing-Tsit Chan, *A Source Book in Chinese Philosophy*, (Princeton: Princeton University Press, 1963).
[4] W. Edwards Deming, "Forces of Destruction," Handout at his seminar, 1990.

- **Emotions**: Joy, pride, delight, fear, anxiety, doubt, trust, despair, hope, happiness, anger, hostility, hatred, love, elation, surprise, anticipation, jealousy, sadness, apathy, security, guilt, courage.

- **Values**: Truth, goodness, beauty, unity, integrity, perfection, uniqueness, necessity, finality, order, justice, simplicity, totality, playfulness, self-sufficiency, self-discipline, self-worth, meaningfulness, creativity, loyalty, faith, service, honesty, centeredness, humility, compassion, accountability, responsibility.

Dr. Deming gives great emphasis to two of these emotions: Joy and Fear. He also speaks of anxiety and courage. Each of us lives these emotions. We feel them deeply. In business we need to operationalize them consistently. To that end, I think that CEO's should write their books or produce their videos before they retire, not after. I think it is extremely important that the CEO expand on the vision and the values and the via that he or she considers important and useful.

Once the CEO clarifies the vision and values, the following process should be useful to help consistently operationalize them. On the next two pages, I provide a list of the resources that you will need and in Figure 6.1, a flow chart which illustrates the methodology you will use.

People: Start with the top leaders in the organization. Then proceed with the others.

Material: A pad of easel paper and a list of decisions that the group has made in the past few months.

A list of values that the group has agreed upon for constancy of purpose in their organization. At General Motors, it is our Beliefs and Values. At Ford, it is their Mission, Values, and Guiding Principles.

Equipment: Black marker.
Masking tape or other wall fastener.

Environment: As free from fear as possible. People must not feel compelled to give the "right" answers.

Method: See flow diagram in Figure 6.1. This flow diagram goes through two cycles of the PDSA that should narrow the gap between the various individual operationalization of values.

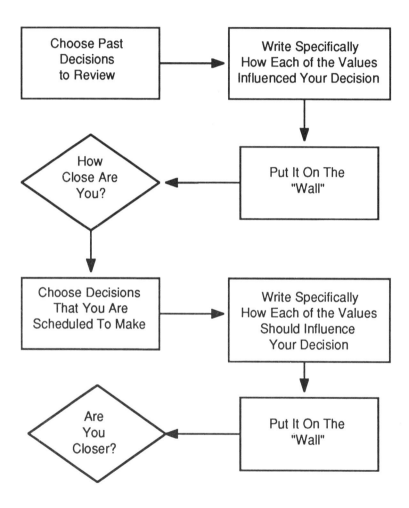

Figure 6.1
Flow Diagram for Improvement

Acknowledge before you start that there will be differences. Try not to be defensive about your interpretation of the values.

First, choose decisions which you all took part in making. If that is not possible, choose group decisions that are as much alike as possible, for comparison.

As future decisions are made, they should be improved because of your closer agreement on the values. Don't become trapped in the morass of an overly precise explanation of your actions. You are trying to come closer together on the *spirit* of the law. Therefore, the values and feelings of the group are far more important than a detailed analysis of facts and rationale.

In Chapter 5, I listed some of the ways that I help others take more joy in what they do. Joy and your need to feel important is very personal: it is within you. Mencius said:

> The desire to be honored is shared by the minds of all men. But all men have in themselves what is really honorable. Only they do not think of it. The honor conferred by men is not true honor. Whoever is made honorable by Chao Meng can be made humble by him again.[5]

I think that leaders can build on these positives by using the framework of Physical, Logical, and Emotional with Independent and Interdependent. You also need to develop ways to reduce the various fears and

---

[5] Wing-Tsit Chan, *A Source Book in Chinese Philosophy* (Princeton: Princeton University Press, 1963).

other negatives that are barriers to people taking joy.
What causes people to be afraid?

> Quite a few people live in constant fear of making
> mistakes. More often than not, the number and
> gravity of their mistakes are no greater than the
> next person's, but this quite evident fact in no way
> mitigates their anxiety. However, their worries
> may indeed make them more prone to commit
> slips and errors, and it is usually their attempts at
> somehow preventing them which set the stage for
> their occurrence.[6]

This is yet another example of Rule 3 of the
Funnel, and it can lead to destruction. Mencius wrote
that when one is affected by fear to any extent, his
mind will not be correct. If his mind is not correct, it
will be difficult to learn.[7] The costs to business, due to
fear, are unknown and unknowable—but they must be
enormous. I am not talking about fear that is external
to a particular organization; like fear of recession or
governmental interference, or the competition. That
kind of fear is relatively easy to harness for quick but
short-lived results. The most destructive fear is that
which is generated inside an organization as a part of
the everyday culture—fear of failure, loss of job, loss of
bonus, loss of respect—all the fears you have observed
(and perhaps experienced) in the workplace.

I am reminded of Herbert Spencer's comment
that it is a sad state of affairs when patriotism is de-

---

[6] Watzlawick, Weakland, and Fisch, *Change* (New York: W.W.
   Norton, 1974).

[7] Wing-Tsit Chan, *A Source Book in Chinese Philosophy* (Princeton: Princeton University Press, 1963).

fined as a common hatred of one's enemies rather than a love of one's country.[8] Company employees who are motivated by fear do make for a "sad state of affairs." But remember, the lack of a negative does not connote a strong positive. To evoke a strong positive emotion, we must operationalize the values that provide us joy.

9

[8]Will Durant, *The Story of Philosophy* (New York: Washington Square Press, 1953).

[9]"RUBES" by Leigh Rubin. By permission of Leigh Rubin and Creators Syndicate.

One kind of fear is generated by one age-old "practice of worship": offering data to the leaders. Certainly the leaders need to know what is happening in their organizations, but fear of failures or mistakes can cause the presenters of data to show nothing but carefully selected good news.

> You have to watch what you say when you're the chairman of a large auto company. Just how much care is required was nicely illustrated in a story they used to tell about General Motors Chairman Roger B. Smith, who reportedly told a private audience that so many people are eager to please a person in a powerful position that it falls little short of crazy. For instance, if Smith off-handedly remarked that he wondered how the GM headquarters building would look painted green, in two hours it would be green.[10]

Corporal punishment (Physical change) is rare today, even in our penal system, but the fear of being punished for your mistakes by being reassigned to the quality control department, or the education and training department, or to be sent on a special assignment, is very much alive today. The threat of that assignment is enough to get many people to avoid taking risks. If you end up in Quality, it is usually a sign that your career is dead-ended (a sad commentary on the status of attitudes toward quality).

Even top quality positions are often only pre-retirement assignments. In spite of the recent talk by prominent CEO's on the importance of quality, change comes very slowly. The position of Chief Quality Offi-

---

[10]Associated Press, James V. Higgins, July 27, 1987.

cer *should* be as desirable as Chief Financial Officer or any other top functional assignment.

**"They put me in charge of special projects.
That means they're still interviewing for my replacement.**

Fear affects a lot of our actions. One recent study of 22 companies found that about 70 percent of employees do not speak up about problems or issues relevant to the prosperity of the company—because of their fear of repercussions.[12]

A similar ritual that propagates fear in the conduct of business is the insistence by "Management for

---

[11]"Selling Short," Ross and Raden, Universal Press Syndicate, 1986.

[12]Ryan and Oestreich, *Driving Fear Out of the Work Place* (San Francisco: Jossey-Bass Publishing, 1991).

No Surprises." This is not a good way to run an organization. It is wasteful and can stifle improvement and spontaneous innovation. "No Surprises" means a lot of pre-work and staffing and posturing so that the meeting, or the report or the decision itself, is a mere formality and anticlimactic (not to mention a waste of time). A "No Surprises" mentality can affect the willingness of a company to change. Even the largest companies today cannot afford a caretaker or a "just-follow-the-procedures" role for management.

All too often, management sees itself solely as the arbiter of the customer, not as the manager of a process that has customers. As a surrogate for the customer, the manager decides that 3 is better than 2; that this drawing is late; that inventory is too high; that sales are too low; that this employee is better than another one. And this is an essential role for the manager to play. It is a Voice of the Customer role. The customer can say that a $3 discount is better than a $2 discount; that this drawing did not arrive in time for me to look at it before the meeting. To the customer, all variation is the same: it is bad. But that is only half of the manager's job. The manager must also listen to the Voice of the Process. This role requires that the manager be coach and counsel, helping the workers develop the process so that it consistently matches the Voice of the Customer.

Management Reporting Processes

I have written and spoken about several management reporting processes that are barriers to continual improvement. Daily Production Reports, the Financial Management Process, and the Personnel Appraisal Process were all covered in my last book.[13] I will update you on the Personnel Appraisal Process later in this chapter, but here I will expand my views on management reporting processes in general.

Managers must choose their questions with care. Questions are cheap; it's the answers that cost organizations a lot of money. But how do you change questions? Through the information you receive. If I can change the management reporting processes, I can usually change the questions that are asked by leaders, and those questions can help change what happens in the organization. In Chapter 5, I listed some useful questions. Others will become more apparent here as I recast some typical management reports.

Change of management processes does not come easily. The introduction of a new process has depended many times on discrediting the process that it is to replace. Continuous improvement can be built on the shoulders of those who have gone before, only if they are standing tall—not rolling over in their graves. Every process that you have today is in place because somebody thought it was the best thing to do for the company (and perhaps for himself as well). You cannot transfer people fast enough to avoid the natural defensiveness of the incumbent if you bring in the new by the discredit of the old.

---

[13]William Scherkenbach, *The Deming Route to Quality and Productivity: Road Maps and Roadblocks* (Washington: CEE-Press, 1987).

Don't get me wrong—I am not advocating the "churning of people." However, you will not be able to truly operationalize continuous improvement until you find a way to build *positively* on what has gone before, and provide a means to save face on things that must go. Actions that are primarily Physical and Logical usually have many stray roots in Emotion.

"My immediate predecessor says he blames his predecessor, and so, by golly, do I blame mine!"

14

The aim of any management reporting process should be to help managers increase joy of ownership through joy of workmanship. To do this, managers need information on the joys that their customers take

---

[14]Source unknown.

in their products and services. They also need information on the joy that their employees take in delivering those products and services to their customers. Any management reporting process must be relevant from the perspective of your customers and also be actionable from the perspective of your employees. Not many processes in industry fulfill both of these requirements. It is usually either one or the other. In the Quality arena you can have:

- audits of final product defects (actionable),
- audits of component level defects (actionable),
- audits of internal customer satisfaction (customer),
- audits of external suppliers (actionable),
- tests for reliability and durability (actionable),
- process for the recall of products (actionable),
- survey of customers for defects (customer),
- process for warranty (actionable),
- process for product development (actionable),
- survey of customers for satisfaction (customer),
- process for the report of internal problems (actionable).

Each of these measurement systems exist because of the questions that your leaders have asked, whether they were proactive and visionary, or reactive to problems. They were not designed to work as a system. And yet they must be. This is the aim of the measurement process that General Motors is piloting. As I said in Chapter 4, each of the 60 measures in the system affects and is affected by other measures.

I think we send a signal on the importance of a process by the reports and information that we request. We sincerely want to convey the message to everyone in the organization that we support quality. We show our sincerity by auditing and asking for reports on the progress we have made in the past month, quarter, and year. We show our desire for quality by making quality performance a part of the bonus equation or a criterion for promotion. Taken independently these are good aims. But taken interdependently as a system, which is what they are, these aims can have very mixed results. I have come to the conclusion that our western culture is one which "manages by scorecard."

If quality is important, put it on the scorecard. If schedule is important, put it on the scorecard. If cost is important, put it on the scorecard. The problem is that you cannot construct a scorecard that will result in overall optimization of the business. Even if you could, that is only one part of what is necessary for change. Scorecards are physical. We need leaders who can make tradeoffs as they make decisions under uncertain circumstances. No set of instructions or scorecards alone will be sufficient. Everyone must understand the logic behind the physical scorecards. If the leaders understand the logic, then they can begin to make the appropriate trade-offs. The leaders also need to have "buy-in," or the will, or the motivation to change. This is emotional—crises are emotional. And crises arise when there is not enough Time or Space to accomplish your aim.

Time

Management is paid to make decisions which affect the future—management's job is prediction. Prediction obviously requires a temporal spread. If your management reports are just "snapshots," you are limiting yourself to a single perspective. Even "driving by looking through the rear view mirror" gives a better perspective, albeit a backwards one. The world of today is not the same as the world of yesterday and even if it was, you have been changed by yesterday's observations. The "temptation in the existing business is always to feed yesterday and to starve tomorrow."[15] How can you put yourselves on a balanced diet? Look at some of the questions and answers that are possible when you look at data over time, balancing the short-term with the long-term view.

Sales by Division

Division	This Month Last Year	This Month This Year
A	40	25
B	26	30
C	20	20

[15]Peter F. Drucker, *Innovation and Entrepreneurship* (London: HarperCollins, 1986).

This typical report of sales by division is misleading to management. First, a comparison of two time periods is not really sufficient for prediction. This is a case where two data points are not necessarily better than one. Through two points, many lines can be drawn.

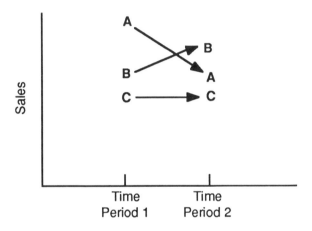

Figure 6.2
Sales by Division: Two Data Points

One of the questions that this report begs to be asked is "Why did the sales in Division A decrease?" Who could blame the manager for asking the question? Last year at this time, the sales were 40; this year they are 25. There must be a reason. Let's look at these data from a different perspective. Look at the sales of Division A for the intervening periods.

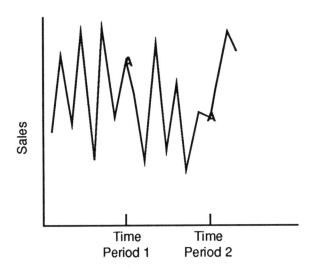

Figure 6.3
Sales by Division: Running Record

What one perspective shows as a decrease in sales, another perspective shows as random variation. With this perspective, an obvious question is "How can we reduce the common cause variation in this sales process?" The answer to this question will lead to improvement.

Let's now look at Division B from a different perspective (see Figure 6.4). One perspective shows an increase in sales, while another perspective clearly shows a decrease in sales on two special occasions.

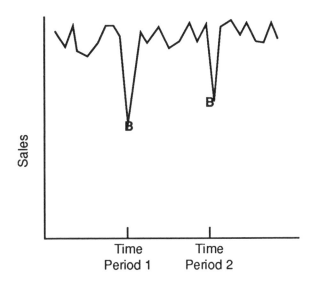

Figure 6.4
Division Sales: A Running Record

Division B has a stable process of sales with very little variation. It is stable with two obvious exceptions. Management might ask "What happened to cause the sales to decrease during these two periods?"

Management (and statisticians) must insist on seeing data over time. Brian Joiner wrote an excellent paper entitled "Lurking Variables."[16] Looking at data over time gives you the following perspectives:

---

[16]"Lurking Variables," Brian Joiner (Madison: Joiner Associates, 1977).

Trends: Do the data gradually drift up or
                   down, over a period of time?

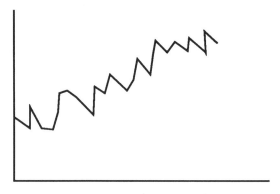

Figure 6.5
Data Over Time: Trends

Shifts: Do the data suddenly go up or down to
                   a particular level?

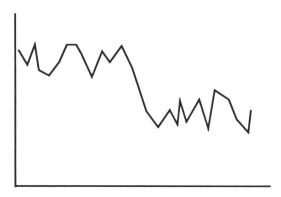

Figure 6.6
Data Over Time: Shifts

Patterns: Are there any seasonal or other physically explainable non-random sequences in the data?

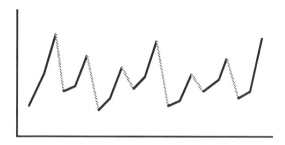

Figure 6.7
Data Over Time: Patterns

Velocity: What is the slope of the trend?

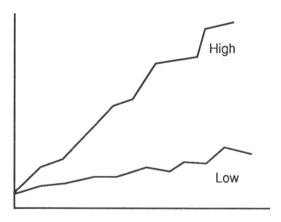

Figure 6.8
Data Over Time: Velocity

Acceleration: How fast are the data changing? Are there any non-linear patterns?

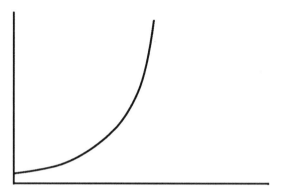

Figure 6.9
Data Over Time: Acceleration

I have experimented with animation techniques for displaying the dynamics of time to decision-makers. I got the idea watching the satellite pictures of moving clouds on the evening news. The first animations were nothing but kinescopes of about 24 graphic snapshots of data. You could see forecasts that pushed the bow wave of optimism just outside the business planning window. While you cannot experience animation in this book, I urge you to try it with your data. Not all data lend themselves to animation; you will have to experiment to see what will be useful to you.

Time, space, Voice of the Customer, Voice of the Process, interdependence, central tendency, and variation are all essential perspectives of a management reporting process. But I do not know of any useful way to include them in one graphic. A graph can quickly become cluttered, with the signal buried in the noise.

You must, however, find a way to display all of these perspectives. What I now use is a portfolio of graphs that link these perspectives. Two of them are a bit unusual. One combines Voice of the Process actuals with Voice of the Customer forecasts. This chart does not have a name, but looks like Figure 6.10.

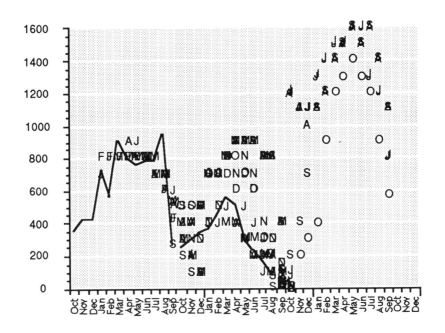

Figure 6.10
Forecasts and Actuals

The solid lines represent the actual sales figures for the month. There seems to be a pattern of sales within a given year: sales build up and then taper down. The number of years shown should be consistent with your long-range planning process. In each month there is also a forecast of sales for that month.

The forecasts were made in each of the preceding 12 to
18 months. Your specific number of forecasts also will
depend on your long-range planning process. Each letter represents the forecast made in a particular month.
For instance, in October of the first year, forecasts
were made for each of the next 12 months. The letters
in the actual graph are color coded to avoid confusion
between months with the same first letter. With this
graphic, you can see the variation of the forecasts for
any given month. For example, in May of the second
year, the sales were forecast to be anywhere from a low
of 300 to a high of 900. With this graphic you can also
see the macro patterns within the year and from year
to year. The level of sales forecasted for the third year
is obviously greater than the previous two years. Is
this a "hockey stick" forecast? What is the special
cause for this change?

Space

I have covered Time—now Space. We suboptimize many times because we do not include enough of
the process as we try to improve it. We gerrymander
the territory in order to win. I think that senior management often acts as if they are legislators, passing
laws that require specific measures to be followed. As
middle management executes these laws, certain loop-
holes are uncovered which are then quickly closed by
senior management. For instance, senior management
might require a new product to be developed within a
budgeted amount of money. It is—taking 6 months
longer than usual to get to market. Senior management then closes the loophole and now requires that
the money target *and* the timing target be met. They

are, of course, but then quality suffers. Senior management now moves to close that loophole, requiring that the cost *and* the timing *and* the quality targets be met. They forget their responsibility to the process that produces the outputs.

Management wants to reduce the cost of doing business. They chose to specify the reduction of the number of salaried personnel. The number of salaried people is dutifully reduced, but in their place temporary workers are used. Management next year closes the loophole by requesting that the number of salaried personnel *and* the number of temporary workers must be reduced. The operations accomplish this by contracting the work to outside companies. Management next year closes the loophole by requesting that the number of salaried personnel *and* the number of temporary workers *and* the number of contracted people must be reduced. This also is accomplished by outsourcing product and the corresponding support work. And on it goes.

The state wants to reduce the tuition charged by the university. It specifies that the university cannot increase its tuition to cover rising costs. The university does not increase tuition but charges students a fee to cover lab expenses. The state moves to close that loophole and says that there will be no increase in tuition *and* no increase in lab fees. The university then begins to charge a library fee. And on it goes.

This headline appeared in the Detroit News and Free Press:

"LOOPHOLE LETS CANDIDATES BEAT SPENDING LIMITS"

The law places several limits on candidates and contributors. (The law limits to $1.5 million the amount the candidates may spend on the election.) But both Democratic Gov. James Blanchard and his GOP challenger, State Senate Majority Leader John Engler, rely on their political parties to help contributors circumvent the restrictions. Instead of writing checks to the candidates or their campaigns, the contributors funnel the money to the parties. The parties then spend the money on behalf of the candidates, a tactic unregulated by law. And on it goes.[17]

The more things change, the more they stay the same. I started Chapter 3 with those words and they apply here in Chapter 6 as well. As Yogi Berra once said, "This is Deja Vu all over again." Peter Drucker relates that the King of Prussia predicted that no one would pay money to ride the new railroad from Berlin to Potsdam in one hour when he could ride his horse for free and get there in one day.[18] A modern day equivalent has an engineering manager who in an attempt to save $80 per person in airfare, put his launch team on a bus. He got his team to their destination, but it took two days to get there. I wonder what it cost for 4 extra days of an engineer's time? What a tradeoff. And on it goes.

A spider diagram is a useful tool to show the tradeoffs that must be made to optimize space. Bass Ale even advertises the numerous subtleties in taste and odor with the use of a "flavour wheel" (see Figure

---

[17]Dawson Bell, Detroit News and Free Press, Nov. 3, 1990.
[18]Peter F. Drucker, *Innovation and Entrepreneurship*(London: HarperCollins, 1986).

6.11). I am very pleased to see that a company which makes a genuine contribution to the betterment of society uses these tools. My grandfather told me "Es gibt kiene schlecht Bier." Of course, now I know that some beers are better than others; there is a distribution.

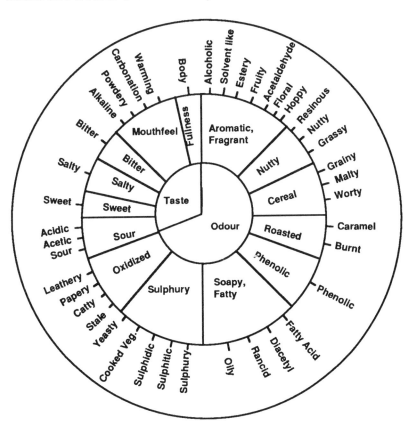

Figure 6.11
The Flavour Wheel[19]

---

[19]A Bass Ale advertisement, Bass Ale Ltd., London.

It is dangerous to manage on the average. If you, as a manager, were shown the chart in Figure 6.12, what question would you ask? You are presented with a chart of cumulative average failures during durability tests of prototypes. You see a trend of improvement in the results of the tests. The tests in 1986 were uniformly better than in 1985 and the tests in 1987 were uniformly better than in 1986.

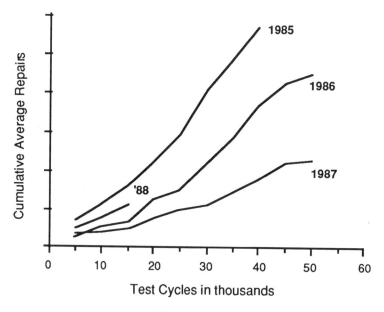

Figure 6.12
Average Repairs by Year

The manager could hardly be blamed for asking "What happened in 1988?" It obviously looks worse than 1986 and 1987. But is it? The above data are averages. A manager needs other perspectives to help make informed decisions. Look at some of the data in the average. The first question that you should ask is "What are the sample sizes in each test group?"

In 1986, five prototypes were tested. In 1988, one prototype was tested. You must know the sample sizes before you can compare averages. If you look at the performance of the individual prototypes tested in 1986, you see a far different picture than if you looked at the average. If you had only the budget to test one, and through luck of the draw you tested either prototype 4 or 5, you would not be program manager any more—you would be looking for another job! On the other hand, if you had tested prototype 1, you still would no longer be program manager. You would have been promoted for your management prowess.

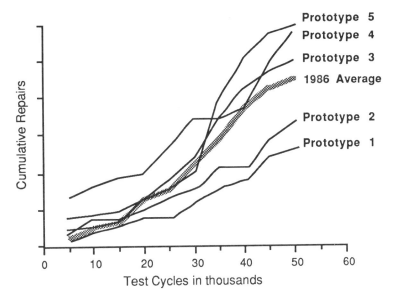

Figure 6.13
Repairs for 1986

If you now compare the individual prototypes in 1986 with the one in 1988, you see that there probably is *no* reason to ask what happened in 1988.

Another Look At the Appraisal Process.

Much has happened in the 4 years since my book, *Road Maps and Roadblocks,* was published. Ford Motor Company has completed its pilot and is implementing a Performance Management Process. General Motors has piloted and is implementing a process entitled Personal Development Plan. Many companies are also beginning the implementation of processes that encourage people to take joy in their work. But we still remain in the beginning stages of what needs to be done.

I will not elaborate on all of the weaknesses of the appraisal process as it exists in many organizations. The weaknesses in Western organizations are different than those in Eastern organizations. For instance, teamwork is a weakness in Western organizations while individual innovation is a weakness in Eastern organizations. As readers, you have gained an awareness of these weaknesses. Indeed, some of you have personal knowledge of them. When Ford changed its appraisal process in the mid 1980's, the Ad Hoc Committee on Performance Appraisal noted several problems with their existing process:

- Lack of balance and perspective
- Short-term emphasis
- Ignored qualitative factors
- Neglected coaching and counseling
- Generally distrusted
- Lack of credibility

I covered all of these, and others, in *The Deming Route to Quality and Productivity: Road Maps and Roadblocks* and in an article in *Quality Progress* entitled "Performance Appraisal and Quality: Ford's New Philosophy."[20] I will elaborate, here on what I think is necessary to help you to do your job. Dr. Deming sees that the aim of leadership should be to improve the performance of man and machine, to improve quality, to increase output, and simultaneously to bring joy of workmanship to people.[21]

What then should be the aim of an appraisal process? It should be to help you help your people take more joy in their work. Specifically,

- it should recognize that people have a right to take joy in their work and it should help them to increase that joy;

- it should recognize that people also strive to be a part of a team and it should help them to increase that sense of joy in family; and

- it should aim to develop and continuously improve people by assisting the leader in the improvement of the process.

---

[20]William Scherkenbach, "Performance Appraisal and Quality: Ford's New Philosophy," *Quality Progress*, Vol. 18, No. 4, 1985.

[21]W. Edwards Deming, *Out of the Crisis* (Cambridge: MIT CAES, 1986), page 248.

People have a right to take joy in their work.

—What will help them take joy in their work?

—How do you know?

—Have you spent the time with them to know?

You must know your people as individual customers. Each of them takes joy in different ways. What stimulates joy in one person is different than what stimulates others. All people respond differently to physical, logical, and emotional cues at various points in time in their lives. At one point in time, more money, vacation, retirement points, a promotion, or a vehicle may stimulate a sense of satisfaction, or joy, in work. At other times, more responsibility, power, or recognition by peers might be needed. Or employees might be concerned with their immortality, legacy, stewardship, or their relationships with others. There is no hierarchy: all of these "rewards" can be equally compelling.

The only way to learn what helps them find joy in work is to spend time with your people. A visit to IBM greatly affected the members of the Ad Hoc Committee at Ford. We asked a cross section of their financial people how much time they spent on coaching, counseling, developing, and other people-related tasks. Their consistent answer was 25 to 30 per cent. This was absolutely incredible to the people at Ford. If we spent 5 percent of our time doing this, it was considered a lot. After all there were questions to answer, fires to fight, costs to cut, problems to solve, and schedules to meet. In fact, the focus of the committee until that visit had been to try to reduce the amount of time spent on the appraisal process. After the visit, we had little trouble convincing the Committee that leaders need to spend more time with their people, not less.

> The vastness of America's territories enabled generations of Americans to solve social problems by escaping from them, instead of working to change them. So long as the frontier beckoned, the sensible way to settle disputes was not painful negotiation, but simply putting some distance between the disputants. American notions of civic virtue came to center less on cooperating with the neighbors than on leaving them alone.[22]

In this process of fight or flight, the country was big enough for the latter option. Even if "this town ain't big enough for the two of us," the country was. Even though "this department ain't big enough for the two of us," the company was. We are in a new economic age; an age where the flight option is rapidly disappearing. Leaders have been able to flee their responsibility to coach and counsel their people. They have been able to avoid the anxiety of dealing with people. I've heard Dean Meyer Feldberg, of Columbia University, observe that in the 1980's it was entirely possible for their graduates to make a lot of money in front of their Quotrons—without ever having to work with people.

Although there is still a need to reduce wasted time and effort in the appraisal process, the time saved should be reinvested with your people.

---

[22]Robert B. Reich, *The Next American Frontier* (New York: Penguin Books, 1984).

—Do you have processes that interfere with joy?

Since different people take joy in different ways, one process might interfere with a person's joy, not affect another's, and positively impact yet another's. For this reason, the process that can have the most negative impact on the joy possessed by your people, is any process that inhibits your flexibility to manage the extrinsic People, Material, Method, Equipment, and Environment so they may be congruent with the Voice of the Customer (in this case, each employee). Many processes limit your flexibility to give only money and promotion, while other extrinsic elements are not even in the realm of possibilities. If you offer more vacation time to someone who would really prefer more on the job training in a skill, you will not help her take more joy in her job. In fact, with this particular loss function, you will probably make the person dysfunctional with the rest of the process.

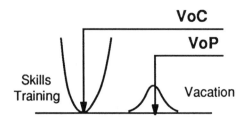

Figure 6.14
Disfunctional Gap in Extrinsic Incentives

If you promote an accountant, who would rather stay an accountant, to a managerial position, you will not help find more joy in his job—in fact, you will probably make him "worse for the reward."

People also strive to be a part of a team.

—Who is on the team?

—Who are their customers?

—Who are their suppliers?

It is relatively easy to consider your team to be the employees who report to you. This is a physical perspective. You need to consider your customers and suppliers to be a part of your team as well. At General Motors, we encourage input and feedback from our internal suppliers and customers. These include our peers, subordinates, supervisors, and people outside of our organization.

Rank ordering people is one of the bigger barriers to teamwork. Much to its credit, General Motors has now abolished rank ordering. The Corporation has stated that, with respect to the compensation program, the Corporate-mandated "forced distribution," and all the terminology that accompanied it, have been eliminated. This change was the result of the strong concern expressed by salaried employees over the detrimental impact forced ranking had on the morale of the organization. Of course, the operational definition of any policy is what results when the policy is implemented, not what was intended. There is still much to be done to reduce this variability in the execution of the policy.

Other features of General Motors' Personal Development Plan include:

—No required ratings

—Multiple input sources should be used

—Methods and results are equally important

—Individual and teamwork are equally important

—Communications and coaching are ongoing

—PDP is linked to other processes, such as compensation.

The leader must continuously develop and improve people.

—Which people?

This question is important because different people will require different kinds of help. The help should be within the framework of the matrix of change and the PDSA improvement cycle. It begins with the selection of your people. "Henry Ford possessed an uncommon gift—or was unusually lucky—in attracting to his company well-educated mechanics who believed that 'work was play.'"[23] As you select employees, you must avoid the tendency to proliferate variation (Rule 4 of the funnel).

If you are able to answer the questions in the other two aims, you are well on your way to helping people improve. "It is better not to make merit a matter of reward lest people conspire and contend, ..."[24]

You must, however *invest* in your people. While you may expect a return on your investment, you do

---

[23]David A. Hounshell, *The American System to Mass Production* (Baltimore/London: University Press, 1984).

[24]Laotzu, *The Way of Life*, trans. Witter Bynner (New York: Perigee Books, 1944).

not treat people like pets, with rewards or punishments for specific performances. Certainly you can *make* anyone do anything. You can make the baby pick up her toys—or the child attend school. You can make a salesperson sell more. You can make people seek reward or avoid punishment. But you will only have accomplished the *letter* of the law, and this is *not enough* to prosper in the new economic age. People must *want* to do the things that you need to have done.

Who should be helped? All people must be helped by the leader, with help tailored to the individual. The help also depends on whether they are inside or outside the system.

—Who is in the system?

If the data show no evidence of special causes of variation, then everyone is considered to be in the system. If you do not have the data, then you might get the people together and ask, "Is there any one of us outstanding in his field?"

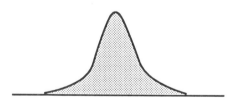

Figure 6.15
All Employees Within The System

If the answer is no, or you begin to argue about it, then debate is cut off and no one is outside of the system. You are all part of the same team. If everyone is inside the system, then a person might be in the top

1% one time and in the bottom 1% another time.
Person 1 has the best performance in April but the
worst in September. This is important information for
the leader to know. It determines whether he can
concentrate on changes that will affect everyone.

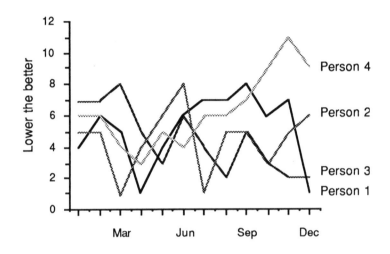

Figure 6.16
Variation of Performance Over Time

—Who is outside the system?

Someone may be outside the system. They can
be outside on the high or low side, or with a special
pattern of performance. This means that they must be
helped in a way that is probably different than the
help that you would give to those inside the system. It
is also important for a leader to know who is not per-
forming in the same system. He knows that he must
learn from these specific individuals to help them as
well as the rest of the system.

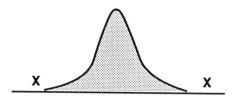

Figure 6.17
Employees Outside the System

—What are the interactions?

> Events in business occur in small measure because
> leaders make decisions; but they occur in large
> measure because the forces of the economy and
> the winds of the market make them so.[25]

Dr. Deming uses the equation $x + y = 8$, where x
represents the contribution of the People and y represents the rest of the process, including Methods, Material, Equipment, Environment, and all their interactions. Even a fifth grader knows that there are many
solutions to that equation. But management has been
carefully taught that $x = 8$. Chapter 1 states that some
processes are People dominant, while others are Material, Method, Equipment, or Environment dominant.
Others are dominated by interactions between the various resources. A manager might invest in the best
technology that money can buy, but if his employees
cannot maintain or operate it, the output will not be
what he expected. There might be positive interac-

---

[25]Peter Koestenbaum, *The Heart of Business* (Dallas: Saybrook
Publishing Company, 1987).

tions between the people and the methods that they use. There might be negative interactions between the equipment and a method of "run it till it drops."

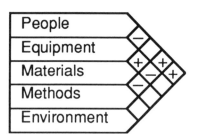

Figure 6.18
Interactions Between Resources

You should not try to "manage on the average," but treat each individual employee as your customer. While this perspective is a necessity, you must balance it with what the *group* of employees think. For this, you must use one of the most misused tools in industry: the survey. My concerns about employee surveys are expressed in one sentence: *Nobody ever seems to take action on the recommendations.* I think the main reason is that the action-takers have not participated in the development of the questions. The action-taker must have ownership of the questions in order to understand the answers, and be motivated to take meaningful action.

The way the survey results are presented can also inhibit action—or cause the leader to misinterpret the results. How would you respond to the following presentation? The pie chart says that only 25% of the people think that *you* are doing a good job. Apart from the fact that it would be very difficult to act on such an ambiguous statement, the verbage in the pie chart hides some very important information.

Figure 6.19
Ineffective Presentation of Survey Results

The survey from which this was excerpted, had five categories for the answers: Very satisfied, satisfied, neutral, dissatisfied, very dissatisfied. The statement that "25% of the employees are satisfied that you are doing a good job" could have been made with any of the following combinations of answers, as shown in Figure 6.20. And the actions you would take in one situation would be completely different from those you would take in another. For instance, if 25% of the employees said that they were very satisfied and 75% of the employees said that they were neutral, you would be a lot better off than if 25% said that they were satisfied and 75% said that they were very dissatisfied.

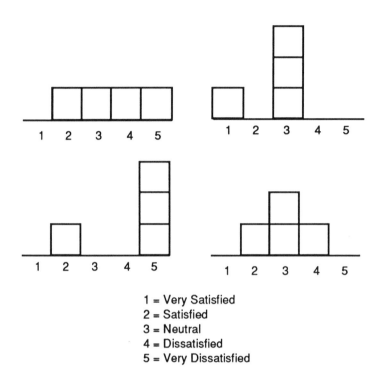

1 = Very Satisfied
2 = Satisfied
3 = Neutral
4 = Dissatisfied
5 = Very Dissatisfied

Figure 6.20
A Better Way of Presenting Survey Results

Some final remarks.

In February 1982, Don Petersen, former chairman of Ford Motor Company, opened a Deming Seminar in February 1982 with these words to some of Ford's most senior executives:

> ... As I was thinking about this meeting, it struck me strongly that you are the ones who are going to decide whether we are really successful in making a dramatic change in how we do business. It can be very difficult

to make significant changes, especially when you have been in the habit of doing things differently for decades, and especially when the very success that brought you to the positions you now hold was rooted in doing some things, frankly, the wrong way. It is going to be hard for you to accept that—that you were promoted for the wrong reasons a time or two.

I seriously suggest that you give that some heartfelt thought as to whether you really understand what we are talking about. I had the experience in January at our Management Review, that most people in the room thought I was talking about something so elementary that we, of course, already do it in the Ford Motor Company. They could not understand why I was talking about it. It left me with the sense that many of us still do not understand what we are really trying to change ...[26]

I wrote this book in part to help you better understand what we are trying to change as well as how to change it.

---

[26]William Scherkenbach *The Deming Route to Quality and Productivity: Road Maps and Roadblocks* (Washington: CEEPress, 1986).

Bibliography

This bibliography contains materials that I consider useful for continual improvement. They have helped me to improve. No book or video mentioned here covers the totality of what this book teaches. It should go without saying that I do not agree with everything written in any of these books. I have found that those who are experts in philosophy, psychology, or engineering have not benefited from statistical thinking. Likewise those experts in statistics or systems optimization have not benefited from the joys of philosophy.

Books or Articles

Brassard, **The Memory Jogger Plus**, GOAL/QPC, Methuen, 1989.

Bridgman, **Philosophical Writings**, Arno Press, New York, 1980.

Bridgman, **Reflections of a Physicist**, Philosophical Library, New York, 1955.

Carlisle & Parker, **Beyond Negotiation**, John Wiley & Sons, Chichester, 1989.

Chambers & Wheeler, **Understanding Statistical Process Control**, SPC Press, Inc., Knoxville, 1986.

Chan, **A Source Book in Chinese Philosophy**, Princeton University Press, 1963.

Deming, **Code of Professional Conduct**, privately published.

Deming, **Elementary Principles of The Statistical Control of Quality**, Nippon Kagaku Gijutsu Remmei, Tokyo, 1951.

Deming, **Out of the Crisis**, MIT Center for Advanced Engineering Study, Cambridge, 1986

Descartes, **Discourse on the Method for Rightly Conducting One's Reason and for Seeking Truth in the Sciences**, Hackett Pub. Co., Indianapolis, 1980.

Gilovich, **How We Know What Isn't So**, The Free Press, New York, 1991.

Gitlow & Gitlow, **The Deming Guide to Quality and Competitive Position**, Prentice-Hall, Inc., Englewood Cliffs, 1987.

Hume, **An Enquiry Concerning Human Understanding**, Oxford University Press, Oxford, 1975.

Ishikawa, **Guide To Quality Control**, Asian Productivity Organization, Tokyo, 1976.

Jessup, **Continuing Process Control and Process Capability Improvement**, Ford Motor Company, Dearborn.

Kane, **Defect Prevention**, Marcel Dekker, New York, 1989.

King, **Better Designs in Half the Time**, GOAL/QPC, Methuen, 1987.

Koestenbaum, **The Heart of Business**, Saybrook Publishing Company, Dallas, 1987.

Kuhn, **The Structure of Scientific Revolutions**, The University of Chicago Press, 1962.

Kuhn, **The Essential Tension**, The University of Chicago Press, 1977.

Latzko, **Quality and Productivity for Bankers and Financial Managers**, Marcel Dekker, New York, 1986.

Laughlin, McManus, & d'Aquili, **Brain, Symbol & Experience**, New Science Library, Boston, 1990.

Leshan & Margenau, **Einstein's Space and Van Gogh's Sky,** Collier Books, New York, 1982.

Lewis, **Mind and the World Order**, Dover Publications, New York, 1929.

Mann, **The Keys to Excellence**, Prestwick Books, Los Angeles, 1985.

McConnell, **Safer Than a Known Way**, Delaware Books, New South Wales, 1988.

McGinnis, **Bringing Out the Best in People**, Augsburg Publishing House, Minneapolis, 1985.

McGregor, **Leadership and Motivation**, The M.I.T. Press, Cambridge, 1966.

Neave, **The Deming Dimension**, SPC Press, Inc., Knoxville, 1990.

Ouchi, **The M-Form Society**, Addison-Wesley, Read-ing, 1984.

Ouchi, **Theory Z**, Avon Books, New York, 1981.

Petersen, **A Better Idea**, Houghton Mifflin Company, Boston, 1991.

Popper, **Objective Knowledge: An Evolutionary Approach**, Revised, Clarendon Press, Oxford, 1989.

Reich, **The Next American Frontier**, Penguin Books, New York, 1983.

Russell, **Introduction to Mathematical Philosophy**, Touchstone Book, New York.

Russell, **The Problems of Philosophy**, Oxford University Press, London, 1959.

Russell, **The Scientific Outlook**, W.W. Norton & Company, New York, 1931.

Ryan and Oestreich, **Driving Fear Out of the Workplace**, Jossey-Bass Inc. Publishers, San Francisco, 1991.

Sagan, **The Dragons of Eden**, Ballantine Books, New York, 1977.

Scherkenbach, **Ford's Major Transition in Continuing Improvement**, Chapter 21 in Productivity and Quality Through People edited by Shetty and Buehler, Quorum Books, Westport, 1985.

Scherkenbach, **Performance Appraisal and Quality: Ford's New Philosophy**, Quality Progress, Vol. 18, No. 4, 1985.

Scherkenbach, **The Deming Route to Quality and Productivity**, CEEPress, Washington, 1987.

Scherkenbach, **The Meaning of Competitiveness**, Quality Data Processing, January, 1988.

Scholtes, **The Team Handbook**, Joiner Associates, Madison, 1988.

Schwinn, **Transformation of American Industry Training System**, PQ Systems, Dayton, 1984.

Shewhart, **Economic Control of Quality of Manufactured Product**, Van Nostrand, New York, 1931.

Shewhart, **Statistical Methods from the Viewpoint of Quality Control**, The Graduate School of the Department of Agriculture, Washington, 1939.

Slote, **Beyond Optimizing**, Harvard University Press, Cambridge, 1989.

Stratton, **An Approach to Quality Improvement That Works**, Quality Press, Milwaukee, 1988.

Tannen, **You Just Don't Understand**, Ballantine Books, New York, 1990.

Tribus, **Deployment Flow Charting**, Quality and Productivity, Inc., Los Angeles, 1989.

Watzlawick, Weakland, and Fisch, **Change**, W.W. Norton & Company, New York, 1974.

Walton, **The Deming Management Method**, Putnam Publishing, New York, 1986.

Western Electric, **Statistical Quality Control Handbook**, AT&T, Indianapolis, 1985.

Wheeler, **Understanding Industrial Experimentation**, 2nd. Ed., SPC Press, Knoxville, 1990.

Videos

The Deming Library, Currently 17 volumes, Films Incorporated, Chicago.

If Japan Can, Why Can't We? - NBC White Paper, Films Incorporated, Chicago.

The Deming of America, Petty Consulting Productions, Cincinnati.

The Batavia Story - Ford Motor Company

Top Management Talks About Quality: Don Petersen, Petty Consulting Productions, Cincinnati.

Roadmap for Change - Britannica

Roadmap for Change II - Britannica

Five Deadly Diseases - Britannica

Windsor Export Supply - Ford Motor Company

The Essential Deming - MIT

Dimensional Control Plan - Ford Motor Company

Statistical Methods and FTQE - Ford Motor Co.

Transformation of American Industry, Tape one - TOAI

The Right Way to Manage - Conway Quality

Quadratic Loss Function - Ford Motor Company

I Know It When I See It - American Management Association

Conversations with Dr. Deming - Ford Motor Company

Conversations with Bill Conway - Ford Motor Company

Permission Citations

Addison-Wesley: William Ouchi, *The M-Form Society*, ©1984 by William G. Ouchi, reprinted by permission of Addison-Wesley Publishing Company.

Clarendon Press, Div. of Oxford University Press: *Parerga and Paralipomena* by Arthur Schopenhauer, translated by E.F.J. Payne (Oxford University Press, 1974).

The Detroit News: Reprinted with the permission of the Detroit News, a Gannett newspaper, © 1991.

Holt, Rinehart and Winston, Inc.: Excerpt from *The Planning of Change*, 4th edition by W. Bennis, K. Benne, and R. Chin, © 1985 by Holt, Rinehart and Winston, Inc., reprinted by permission of the publisher.

Harper Business: *From the Borderless World*, by Kenichi Ohmae, © 1990 by McKinsey and Company, Inc. Used by permission of Harper Business, a div. of HarperCollins Pub.

Houghton Mifflin Co.: *No Contest: The Case Against Competition* by Alfie Kohn. © 1986 by Alfie Kohn, Reprinted by permission of Houghton Mifflin Company.

King Features: *Willy 'n Ethel,* © 1991 by King Features Syndicate, Inc. World Rights Reserved. Reprinted with special permission of King Features Syndicate, Inc.

Laughlin, McManus, & d'Aquili, **Brain, Symbol & Experience**, New Science Library, Boston, 1990. Reprinted here by arrangement with Shambhala Publications, Inc. 300 Massachusetts Ave. Boston, MA 02115.

MIT: Reprinted from *Out of the Crisis* by Dr. W. Edwards Deming by permission of MIT and Dr. W. Edwards Deming. Published by MIT Center for Advanced Engineering Study. Cambridge, MA 02139. © 1986 by W. Edwards Deming.

Science News: Reprinted with permission from Science News, the weekly newsmagazine of science, © 1990 by Science Service, Inc.

John Wiley & Sons: *Sample Designs in Business Research* by Dr. W. Edwards Deming. © 1960. Reprinted with permission from John Wiley & Sons, Inc.

Ziggy, copyright Ziggy and Friends. "Selling Short," dist. by Universal Press Syndicate. Reprinted with permission.

Index of Figures

Index

Additional Copies of this book
may be ordered directly from:

SPC Press, Inc.

5908 Toole Drive, Suite C
Knoxville, Tennessee   37919

Telephone	(615) 584-5005
Fax Number	(615) 588-9440
Toll-free Order Line	**1-800-545-8602**

Price	$ 32.00
Shipping & Handling	2.50

(Tennessee Customers add 8.25% Sales Tax)

Other titles are available.
For a free catalogue, write or call SPC Press.